All My Life as a Bubble

By Theo Philippou

The following story is true: all the contents are based on actual events, some character names have been changed in accordance with copyright laws.

1990

Late evening on a cold foggy October night and I was contemplating what course of evasive action I might take in order to extract myself from a deteriorating and life threatening situation.

Two tall skinny young black men had pulled hankies up around their mouths and noses, their partial disguises added malicious intent to the attack that they so desperately wanted to carry out.

The two criminals were shrouded by the evening fog and anyone walking past or driving by from a distance would not see them, I could see them very clearly . . . they stood beside me with their backs on either side of my stationery vehicle as they attempted to open my two front doors without even a glance towards me.

They lifted the silver slotted handles of the *Ford Cortina* expecting the doors to open and allow them entry and access; to me!

People make several mistakes in life and I had made several in my thirty six years . . . but becoming a mini cab driver was a short term job I had taken on in an attempt to pay the bills and put food on the table for my wife and two young children.

As you may have realised my taxi career had not gone very well.

A well to do gentleman had hired me via the office of a Streatham mini cab business. He was a large well dressed man in his early thirties and he reminded me very much of *Mr T* . . . the character in *The A Team,* Smartly dressed in fine clothing, a Fedora hat and a thick solid gold chain that hung around his wide neck and his broad chest.

It was eight pm as we set of from Wellfield Road in Streatham; I asked him for his destination please?

"My man . . . " He said with gusto,

". . . Take me to the Front Line. I want you take me there, wait for me and bring me back,"

My heart sank; Railton Road, Brixton was at that time notorious for the small dens that peddled narcotics to anyone who had the money and going by my customer's enthusiasm it looked like he was looking for a piece of that illegal action.

At times you get strange intuitive warning vibes don't you? Well I was getting a massive feeling of foreboding.

I had worked on into the evening because takings had been low, usually I would have been at home at that time relaxing with my wife Rita and two adorable young children Alex and Reanna.

Instead I was on a journey to hell but hopefully on a return journey back!

"Stop here" *Mister T* instructed.

He clambered out of the front passenger seat and after the door slammed shut I instinctively pushed all the black peg locks down.

An uneasy feeling of discomfort kept prodding, I felt the urge to start the engine and get the hell away from a fog ridden south east London street which would have blended in well with a *Jack The Ripper story* . . . and all of a sudden there they were, these two knife carrying masked muggers that would show me no mercy . . . and it worried me immensely that if they got inside the car and realised that there was actually not enough money there to buy them even a pack of cigarettes each then surely they would dish out an intense frenzied anger on moi.

Self preservation kicked in as I turned the ignition key and thankfully . . . the old Cortina started straight away . . . I drove away from them and turned directly onto the grand old Railton Road.

There were more street lights on the 'front line' as the two would be muggers melted away into their little bolt holes.

So being a stupid person I decided to stop by one of those street lights and await the return of *Mister T.*

About twenty minutes passed, twenty minutes of checking mirrors and keeping the engine running; in case I needed a quick getaway.

The two men reappeared and began walking up behind my vehicle, that was it . . . I had made a decision . . . 'Good by Railton Road, I am out of here.'

And then he appeared . . . .

Mister T was on the move, he had almost fallen out of an all night liquor store and he was running for his life . . . his expensive camel hair coat flapped around him as he shouted out to me in a panic stricken voice . . .

"Wait . . . wait . . . . wait for me"

Fuck!

I mean, what do you do?

What should I do sitting there amongst knife wielding muggers on a foggy 'front line' with a man running towards me yelling at me to wait, when during all of that wasted time it had been my very intention to wait but now he was in obvious danger and running, seemingly for his life . . . that really worried me . . . *should I stay or I should I go?*

Mister T had covered twenty five metres of the fifty metres distance from the shop to my car in record time.

Unfortunately for him . . . four men were running after him, they were attempting to grab him as he sprinted towards me.

His urgent unheralded and out of breath arrival at my passenger door panicked my two would be muggers who both took a step back.

I now realise that it was probably the sight of the four pursuers that had worried them even more and thinking about it now: the four men were probably higher up the gangster captaincy food chain than their own petty criminal ratings.

It was surreal and I just stared at Mister T as he shouted at me,

"Open the door . . . Open the door?"

The door was still locked, I calculated that I had time to open the door, let him get one leg inside and then I would drive away . . . at speed.

Mr T got into the car but my calculations were incorrect.

His four pursuers had caught up with him and he did a stupid thing . . . I heard myself shouting at him amidst all of the other threatening shouts,

"What are you doing?"

Mr T leant over his seat and . . . unlocked the door behind him.

Three of the four large men; of West Indian decent all squeezed into the back of my car and that is the first and so far only time that I perceived myself as plummeting helplessly into the flames of hell and evil.

Their obvious leader and the only one who spoke held a large gleaming machete up in front of his face and jabbed it repeatedly towards *Mr T*

Mister T pleaded,

"C'mon man what is all this . . . you know me" He tried to sound calm.

The machete man replied in a thick Jamaican twang,

"Yeah, respect friend . . . but you need to understand"

"What . . . tell me" Asked *Mr T.*

"It's like this man . . . I need thirty dollars."

Mr T breathed out a sigh of relief as he said,

"Well why didn't you say, here man take this,"

He gave the machete man three ten pound notes.

The man muttered his thanks and within three seconds, thankfully . . . and I thank God to this day . . . they got out of my car.

I swung away from the pavement and sped down Railton road as Mr T closed his door and shouted,

"Drive man . . . drive . . . get us out of here"

My life had been in danger and I had probably saved Mr T from a blood thirsty murder as without a getaway vehicle, the vultures would more than likely have cleansed him of all his money and much more.

I gave up being a taxi driver a few years later and do not miss it now in the slightest.

It was an incident that I will always remember but the thing that really saddened me about that night is that it occurred in Brixton, a place where I had enjoyed many happy childhood memories.

1962

During the sixties, Sundays were special days for everyone not just Greek Cypriots, a Sunday was truly the only day of relaxation as Sunday trading was illegal and it worked out, that for at least one in every three Sundays we would be invited to a Greek Wedding which; we always attended.

The young immigrant Cypriot community ensured an abundance of new marriages which were popular crowded events, and because everyone came from the tiny island of Cyprus all the guests were either related or knew someone who was with someone else and it all came back around in a muddled friendly circle.

At the age of six I was conscious of other people looking on from buses or walking past and staring at this mass gathering of people all trying to get inside the small Greek Orthodox churches of London while talking in Greek and in typical Cypriot fashion talking very loudly.

I liked to observe these wonderfully exaggerated mannerisms, the extravagantly passionate hugs (which incidentally had to be instrumental in paving the way for the now modern body bumping hugs and kisses that are common - place between all teenagers) and the Churches - those wonderful archaic deeply religious houses of God.

Even now I can recall the smell of frankincense mixed in with the melted wax fumes that were released by the giant flickering church candles. The holy lanterns were shaken around by Priests dressed ceremoniously in their long gold coloured cloaks; long bearded Orthodox priests who chanted religious psalms as they shook their gold plated lanterns up and across the church aisles.

The actual Church ceremonies were long drawn out affairs, too long for impatient little six year olds like me but thinking back now I guess they were quite spectacular.

The Wedding receptions were amazing. The fact that the bride's parents were poor or wealthy was irrelevant. Specially hired halls were laid out by expert caterers – who were always Greeks and filled with Greek buffet's consisting of meatballs, stuffed vine leaves, Greek Macaroni cheese, chicken legs, roast potatoes and other Cypriot food.

Or sometimes a sumptuous silver service banquet was laid on by the wealthier Greek families that wanted to show us how well they had done. We were spoilt by a' La Carte menu's accompanied by ample alcohol for adults and fizzy drinks for the likes of yours truly.

All of them were a truly scrumptious affair and all of them had authentic Live Greek bands that included expert Bouzouki guitar strings and ace violinists, they all authenticated the Greek atmosphere and of course, heralded the famous Greek money - pinning wedding dance ceremony.

(How could anyone have ever imagined in a million years that when I grew up and got married that my very own daughter would be the star of the *BBC'S Don't Tell the Bride* and a pretty good version of a Greek Wedding but without the church bit as the ceremony was held on The H.M.S. Belfast)

I suppose you could say that whilst I disapproved of all these weddings taking up part of my child hood I was in a way addicted to them.

Once I was there, I would look for the same pretty twenty year old Greek girls who made all the right moves as they swayed perfectly to every dance arms held high and extended outwards in tune to the live Greek music as they snapped their fingers rhythmically to accompany the quick crisscrossing of their feet.

Others would join in and the handkerchiefs would be flipped flamboyantly as two people grabbed a corner each of the hankie and jerked it around the dance floor in rhythm to the bouzouki with a flamboyant slap of their heel or a high kick as they cheered "Opah"

It irked me somewhat that I could not dance then, at the age of six, (nor now) and it also made me wonder why, every time I saw these dancers, my father and mother and others would join in with the dancing without inviting me to dance with them.

It was at one such wedding in North London that my father made the acquaintance of a smartly dressed Jewish gentleman, Mister Margot, who along with his wife had been seated at our table. Mister Margot and my father had been in the midst of a long in depth conversation about something right up until when food was served.

While we were sat there eating our wedding food, a tall overweight unshaven Greek man I had never seen before approached my father.

I saw him first as he marched up behind my father and slapped him heartily on the back;

"George - you son of a gun"

My father smiled as he felt the friendly slap, but as he turned to face the visitor, the smile on his face vanished when he recognised his old acquaintance.

"Nick, hi..." My dad George forced himself to smile.

"..Good to see you Nick." I heard him say but my father looked far from pleased.

Well that was it, the invitation 'the good to see you' was all Nick needed.

To my horror Nick grabbed the chair my mother was sitting on and with her still seated inside the chair he dragged her aside.

My mother was too flabbergasted to say a word as Nick grabbed a vacant chair and squeezed into the newly vacated space.

Mister Margot and his wife tried to be polite by looking away from Nick and my father.

Nick leaned closer towards my father George and began to confide in him.

"George, George, what a fucking time, I swear, it was fucking hell those idiots, the faggots in there and the moron's my god, I thought I would kill myself. Luckily I managed to bribe a couple of the Prison Guards you know with the stuff my mother Elene smuggled into me every week and that helped me out a bit, thank god, three fucking years George, three years."

Now, I did not know about prison life, nor had I heard any English blasphemy until then, but believe me, my little ears pricked up as I watched Nick the Greek open up his heart to my father who I must admit looked like he wanted to be somewhere else at that moment in time.

"Okay Nick ..." My father said,

"..But you're okay now, you are a free man Nick and it's good to see you."

Nick held up a hand like a stop sign, meaning stop talking George 'what I have to say next is really important.'

"She's here George, she is here my Sophia. My darling wife Sophia is here, but she won't talk to me George, God I missed her so much.

She never visited, not once George but now I am free she won't even come near me."

Nick looked as if he was about to start sobbing and I have to admit that it was about then that I began to dislike his selfish self pity.

Nick slammed the flat part of his large hand on the table cloth, there was a loud muffled bang and the cutlery on our table jumped and clattered startling everyone around us.

My father tried to calm him.

"Nick, you have to give her time, after all Nick you did try and kill her. You really ought to be more reasonable."

Nick the Greek seemed to become agitated by my father's comment. He waved his hands with true Greek animated efforts to express his torment.

"Reasonable George, you got to be fucking kidding me, reasonable? I just wasted three fucking years of my life because of her. I will tell you what's reasonable George, here take a look at this."

With his left hand Nick pulled the left hand side of his jacket away from his chest and allowed my father to catch sight of a shiny black gun stuck inside his waist band.

My father's face acquired a very pale complexion.

"Christ Nick, what are you doing?" He gulped.

"I don't care George, if she won't have me back, I will kill her, right here, right now." This kind of passionate temperament was pretty usual for us Greeks and I found my curiosity latching on to his Greek tragedy but the sight of the pistol was pretty scary.

My father grabbed Nick's arm and forced him to cover up the gun by making Nick let go of the jacket.

He pulled Nick to his feet and away from our table.

The two men entered into an intense discussion before Nick turned away from my father and stormed out of the wedding hall.

*   *   *

The place was new to me, I was six years of age and with my sister Androulla, who was one year older. We had been taken by our parents to a restaurant in Kennington an area near Westminster in London. It was a new experience for us as we were usually a stay at home family who, apart from Sunday weddings, rarely ventured out. It felt strange to be socialising with our father George; a handsome young Greek man in his mid – twenties someone who we seldom saw unless he finished work earlier than usual at one of London's high class restaurants where he worked as a head waiter and; my mother Effie, light skinned and beautiful with long tumbling wavy brown hair that made her look like a Hollywood starlet she was so photogenic that in her teenage years a scout for a leading shampoo company had offered her a modelling contract.

In his strong Greek Cypriot accent George talked the best he could in broken English with the owner of the restaurant - the same Mister Margot we had met at the Greek Wedding and they seemed to be celebrating something as they shook hands heartily.

My sister Androulla and I were unaware that this visit had followed weeks of negotiations by our father to secure the purchase of the restaurant.

From that cold day in February my family became the owners of the quaint medium sized restaurant on the corner of Brook Drive and Kennington Road, South London. A venture that would result in more twists and turns than the year's current hit by Chubby Checker *Let's Twist Again*.

George quickly put his entrepreneurial skills to use.

The old fashioned café name was changed and the restaurant became known as; The Oasis.

The opening hours changed, instead of closing at six pm the restaurant closed every Monday to Saturday at eleven pm and that was when the face of London's night life extended itself southwards across the river Thames and into The Oasis Café in Kennington.

Uncles and aunts I had never met turned up to work at The Oasis. Experienced caterers who ensured George and Effie's menu could be cooked and delivered to the many customers that frequented the Oasis.

Business thrived.

Most of the time my sister and I were despatched to an old settee in the living room above the café where I often fell asleep only to wake up the next morning at our home in Streatham Hill as my mother prepared us for school and then - my big seven year old sister Androulla would take my hand and lead me or sometimes drag me on our long walk to our infant's school *Hitherfield* in West Norwood.

When we were at the café during school holidays we were allowed to play in Harmsworth Park, which happily was directly across the road from the café and which, to my absolute delight and jubilation is home to The Imperial War Museum.

So that's what this little six year old would do every week day after being picked up from school, I would go with my sister Androulla or on my own and visit the Imperial War Museum . I would walk around viewing the exhibits for what seemed like hours staring at the glass display cases that housed treasures which made the imagination of a child leap into so many exciting and different worlds.

I was fascinated by the intricate fine detailed war scenes that had been laid out on carefully crafted battle fields. The attention to detail was painstaking and I or any one else that was privileged enough to have viewed those exhibits would have been in awe of the craftsmen who had made the authentic First and Second World War battle scenes; the trenches at the battle of The Somme and the tank battles across Arabia. You really could see the tiny model soldiers screaming in agony from their bayonet wounds as one became immersed in the ages recent and distant that the museum remembered with meticulous detail.

One summer's day I was gifted another magical dreamland. As I walked into the café I immediately noticed the new arrivals, a long high pinball machine had been plugged into a wall socket, it flashed and whirred like the star attraction at a fairground. Believe me, for a six year old, nothing comes closer to paradise than such a sight and to nearly equal that, the icing on the pinball machine was the other new addition; The Juke Box.

So I went from being a curly haired dopy little Greek Cypriot kid with dirty knees and a snotty nose, to, a curly haired dopy little Greek Cypriot Kid with dirty knees and a snotty nose, who had acquired his own real life adventure comic in the shape of The Imperial War Museum and I was also blessed with a whirling, pinging, all action pinball machine and to top it all; rock n roll music, how lucky was I?

During the following weeks, several warnings and ticking offs were handed down to me by my parents because of my insistence to stand on a small wooden Schweppes drinks box in order to elevate my height and to help me stretch my little arms around the edges of the pinball machine so that I could just about reach the red flipper buttons.

Eventually I was admonished and unsuccessfully barred from trying to play the pinball machine because; they said I was in danger of tripping up customers with my little box.

Thinking back it must have been an annoying sight.

Saturday afternoons were the most tedious as my father George and his cousin and two brother in laws, all in their late twenties would go up to the sitting room - move all the furniture to one side and wrestle violently with each other - wrestle with such force that my mother would remonstrate with them over the noises the crashing body slams and nose bleeding forearm smashes were creating for diners in the restaurant below; who in turn could hear the loud crashing sounds and watch the ceiling above them buckling. So I would sneak out and visit my museum until hopefully, wrestling time was over.

The arrival of the juke box coincided with the arrival of The Mod's.

In the early sixties some teenagers were fashionably either Rockers or Mods.

Rockers were the leather clad motorbike Hell's Angel's followers and Mods were the parker coated *Lambretta* Scooter riders who all seemed to be male and who all seemed to carry pretty female riders that hugged their waists as they drove up with a controlled bump onto the pavement outside our Oasis Café.

My little eyes were agog as I watched dozens and dozens of Mods pull up every evening and all of them without doubt to frequent my mum and dad's café.

The Oasis very quickly became The Mod centre of South London.

The Juke Box blared out famous hits and at times there was not a spare seat to be found anywhere amongst the eighteen red laminate topped tables each with their accompanying six chairs and I just kept on walking out there in the midst of them, just to stare at all those pretty girls but I was always yanked back into the kitchen.

It was great even though at the time I was much too young to realise that I was privileged enough to be living the sixties dream in amongst the dream sixties generation.

One Friday evening I watched the diners as they enjoyed each other's company. They joked and enthused over what must have been interesting topics.

A pop tune exploded out of the juke box and to my surprise a young couple that I had noticed before; David and Susan, jumped to their feet and began dancing to the tune, it was called; *Let's Dance, by Chris Montez*. I had never seen such excitement at the café, some applauded as others cheered and David and Susan were brilliant at dancing with one another, so good that when my father ran out of the kitchen to see what all the fuss was about he too stopped and watched.

We were both captivated as the couple showed off their perfect moves and when David held Susan's hand above her head and twirled her in a pirouette Susan's skirt flared up like an umbrella revealing her perfect slender legs all the way up to her waistline. It was mesmerising stuff.

The song finished as David embraced Susan and kissed her on the lips, more cheers from their friends and then a gentle warning from my father George that there was to be no more dancing in his café.

It was during that evening that I once again sneaked out with my little wooden drinks box and inserted a sixpence into the coin slot of the pinball machine - I loved the clunking noise the little silver pinball made as it shot up into the launch aisle as the whirring and flickering noises announced: game on.

I was in the best place ever, about to play my pinball machine.

Unexpectedly my feet came away from the wooden box, I was hovering in mid - air - I had floated upwards by at least two feet, the pinball machine was out of my reach as I kicked my legs and tried to get back on a firm footing.

I felt an uncomfortable squeezing of skin on the back of my neck.

Someone had grabbed me from the back of my shirt collar and lifted me away from the pinball machine, I was being flown back towards the kitchen as customers stared and laughed at me, I was taken through the entrance to the kitchen and lowered back on to the floor.

It was probably the first time I had felt anger as I turned to face my assailant and when I looked up and saw him, I was lost for words - it was Nick the Greek.

"Your father has told you time and again, no Pinball table, do you understand me?"

I think I pissed in my little pants as I ran up the stairs to the spare room not at all happy with the fact that Nick the Greek had been recruited to work at the Oasis.

The next day, during a late Saturday afternoon I went with my sister to play in Harmsworth Park and as I ran towards the two huge fifteen inch naval guns that loomed ceremoniously outside the Imperial War Museum I stopped as I spotted David and Susan sitting on one of the park benches.

I saw that they were in the midst of a serious conversation, David was pleading he looked upset as Susan turned her head away from him, she looked sad.

Susan noticed me standing nearby staring at them, her beautiful blue eyes seemed to sparkle as she gave me the most wonderful brief smile just as David grabbed her arm, and forced her to look back at him.

I moved away and went into the museum.

My attention was captured by the overhanging Japanese Zero fighter planes and I heard a museum guide telling visitors how destructive the planes had been during the war with their kamikaze missions.

How ridiculous is fate and how strange are coincidences: Several years later whilst on a business meeting to measure some apparatus I returned to the Imperial War Museum for the very first and last time at the age of forty six and when I finished my calculations . . . I went and stood in that chamber and looked up at the Zero's; they were still hanging in the air . . . and it was at that precise hour on that very day that the Nine Eleven hijackers kamikazed themselves and their helpless passengers into the first of the New York Trade Towers.

*   *   *   *

Saturday night, the busiest night of the week, the Oasis was fully staffed, there had been a steady stream of customers from seven pm.

At one stage the food orders were at such a high volume; I was made to stand on my little wooden Schweppes box by the large square white sink and wash dishes next to my sister Androulla who kept reminding me that I was hopeless at washing up.

She was right.

I sneaked back into the crowded restaurant.

It was so busy that my parents who were both at the counter taking money and orders, did not notice me or perhaps, chose to ignore me.

I looked at the tables, all fully seated except for one where a young man I had never seen before sat on his own staring out of the window on to the Kennington Road. It seemed to be a shame that all those spare seats at his table were being wasted so I watched to see if other people would eventually join him at his table.

It was at about nine o clock that I noticed the arrival of David and Susan.

They were laughing and joking as they entered with two of their friends and waited patiently for a vacant table.

By chance, as their teas were placed on the counter four other people vacated a nearby table. David and Susan and their friends shuffled across to occupy the area.

I was pleased to see that David and Susan were in a happy mood.

Susan was chatting happily to her girlfriend and David was talking to the other young man, but they did not notice the man who had earlier taken up a whole table on his own begin to stare at them with a horrible angry look in his eyes.

I knew there was something strange about the man's demeanour, he looked annoyed and fixated my little eyes widened as I saw the man pick up a chair and raise it above his head.

I think I shouted,

"No"

But it was too noisy for anyone to hear me.

The man swung the chair and struck David across the back of his head.

Screams and cries of anguish erupted from Susan and her friends as David fell to the floor.

The man stood and stared at Susan, she looked up at him, for a second I thought she would attack the man who I later found out by eavesdropping in on several conversations that it was her previous boyfriend, Simon but Simon turned away from her and ran out of the café.

Pandemonium is a good Greek word to describe what happened next, no one inside the café knew what to do, other than scream and shout until my father George and Nick the Greek vaulted over the service counter, right in amongst everyone - my father shouted at them,

"Everyone be quiet, stop screaming."

They ignored him.

Nick the Greek Held up the biggest meat cleaver anyone would wish to see in that type of situation;

"Shut up all of you." He ranted.

His warning brought about an immediate silence.

I saw two girls and one boy faint.

"Right..." my father warned them, with a strong Mediterranean accent,

" . . . Everyone get in a queue against the window, now." They stared at my father.

Nick the Greek, waved his meat cleaver.

"Do it, now" Nick shouted.

All the customers, who were absolutely petrified, formed the most orderly queue I have ever seen as, one by one and without saying a word they filed out of the front door.

I can recall the weird experience of watching them exit one by one as my father George stood silently next to Nick the Greek and the meat cleaver and while all this was going on, the Juke Box tune that was playing clearly and smoothly was; *I Can't stop loving you*, by *Ray Charles*.

I glanced to the floor where David had fallen, he had gone.

I looked around and spotted David standing outside on the pavement; tiny rivers of blood flowed down every part of his face. I saw a passing motorist stop his car and bundle David into the rear passenger seat and then quickly drive him to the nearby St Thomas' hospital accident and emergency unit.

It was a sad evening and soon after, due to understandable concerns from my mother, the café was put up for sale.

The evenings at the Oasis café became shorter as the closing times were cut from eleven to six pm and eventually my family moved on, but not before I had the chance to visit my Museum a few more times and on one of those visits, I spotted David and Susan sitting happily on their park bench, kissing and cuddling, It made me smile. I was also pleased that they noticed me and especially pleased when the beautiful Susan blew me a tiny kiss from the cup of her hand which struck directly at the centre of my little heart.

*   *   *

1960. Madaba - Jordan.

 Seventeen year old May was in love and she was thrilled that the nineteen year old boy she was smitten with was now working alongside her in her father Yaseen's general store.

 They had known each other through their early school years and then later during their senior classes, their friendship blossomed into a romantic appreciation for each other yet her strict upbringing meant that up until that day in the store - May had never been left alone with any man who might have threatened her virginity with even the slightest hint of a smile let alone romance.

 Yaseen had raised his only child alone since his wife had died giving birth.

 On this particular day however Yaseen needed to attend an important meeting with his bank manager. He asked Adam to keep a protective eye on the shop and informed his daughter almost too persuasively that he would, 'Return within twenty minutes, maximum.'

 May kept her head low as Yaseen sped away in his old battered truck.

When he had driven out of sight, she raised her head.

Adam grinned, he liked the fact that May was blushing he walked over to May and for the first time they kissed.

*   *   *

The two prisoners had been on the run for two days.

They were exhausted and hungry. Their unshaven faces had suffered burns from the intense heat of the searing Sun and their throats had become swollen due to the lack of hydration.

Khaled and Saeed had escaped from the notorious Al Jafr prison.

The misfortune of another prisoner who had hung himself, had given them the tiniest window of opportunity to escape whilst four prison guards struggled to cut down the overweight suicide victim's body.

Khaled and Saeed ran through the open gates that the ambulance had passed through and they had kept on running until that point; the point where they had entered the outskirts of Madaba and stumbled across the secluded shop which appeared brighter and bigger than any mirage they could ever wish for.

The shop door swung open and the two men entered, May and Adam immediately sensed danger, the men's appearances and their body language threatened a multitude of evils.

Adam stepped forward.

"We are just about to close" He lied.

Saeed who was nearest to the door looked around the store and then at Adam before looking at May.

"Are you two here alone?" He asked in a gruff voice.

"Sorry, we are closed you will have to leave, right now please." Adam said politely but firmly.

Saeed shut the door, he locked it with the key that was in the door and turned over the sign that read on the one side open and the other closed he pulled down the door's roller blind, obscuring any view from the street outside. He walked over to a display storage rack and from it he lifted out a pick axe handle with its special offer tag still attached.

Khaled walked up to the teenagers and slammed his hand noisily on the counter.

"Get us some water, now."

May looked to Adam and nodded.

"Okay, no problem I will get you water, relax." She said calmly.

"Saeed, go with her" Khaled shouted.

Saeed walked over quickly, he grabbed May by the arm.

Adam shouted,

"Hey" and rushed forward to protect her.

Saeed swung his arm and struck Adam across the forehead with the thick end of the pick axe handle.

Adam fell to the ground as May screamed,

"Please, stop, I will get your water, please, don't hit him anymore there is no need." She cried.

Adam groaned as he sat on the floor holding his head. May ran into the back scullery and returned within seconds carrying a jug of water and three glasses. She placed the three glasses on the shop counter and filled them with the water.

May then took one of the filled glasses over to Adam, she soaked a cloth in the water before dabbing it over Adams bruised head.

May turned slowly towards the intruders and shouted defiantly,

"There, drink your water and then get out."

Khaled and Saeed gulped down the water, re-filling three times, spilling water over their faces and onto the floor.

They stared at the two teenagers.

"Listen, to me." Saeed said to May calmly.

"We mean you no harm, we just need some food and money and we will be gone, you understand?"

Khaled interrupted,

"And a wash and change of clothing, you have everything here, it won't take long."

"My father is due back soon, if he finds you here he will call the police, you do not have time to wash or change."

May stood up and walked over to the cash register she opened the draw and took out the Dinar's.

"Here, money, take it." She placed the paper money on the counter.

She took a large basket and quickly filled it with bread, cheese and fruit. She slammed the basket on to the counter next to the money.

"Here, food. Now take it and get out."

Saeed stared at May.

"You have a nasty attitude, you little whore, who do you think you are talking to? Do you know who I am?"

"I do not care, just get out, now."

Khaled took the basket and the money from the counter, he nudged Saeed.

"Saeed let's go now. We have what we want, come."

Khaled stared at May and reluctantly he conceded.

The two men walked over to the door, Adam stood up and walked over to May's side, they watched in silence as Saeed turned the key in the lock and opened the door.

As the door opened, May and Adam saw the armed police officers lining the street opposite, there were too many policemen to count and they were all pointing rifles and guns at the store.

Saeed and Khaled saw them as well, but there was little time for them to turn or run as the police let rip a salvo of bullets.

The slaughter continued for at least thirty seconds as both escaped convicts absorbed a savage volley of ammo that shredded them from their outsides through to their insides, they shook violently before falling to the floor dead. The windows of the store disintegrated from the volley of gun fire.

May was struck by a bullet in her left eye and Adam was shot twice in his stomach and once in his neck, he was dead before he hit the ground.

May collapsed and fell to the floor beside him.

*   *   *

1961 Hitherfield School - West Norwood, London

It was the first time I had heard a school bell ring.

I felt I would cry as I left my mother standing with the other parents who also looked concerned yet proud.

My attention was held by the dozens of children that had been running around the playground, laughing and playing, I was enthused by their enjoyment and I wanted to join in with the fun of school.

My name, along with others was called out and we were led to our class rooms.

In my class, all thirty of us were designated our own little table to sit behind.

The teacher kept asking us questions that even I understood, I was very keen to participate in the lady teachers questions and answers session, so, every time she asked something, my little hand shot up and when she asked me for my answer I blurted out a quick response, but, for some reason the other children giggled at me.

I could not understand why and reached my own conclusion that they must have found me, rather entertaining.

She asked another question, I raised my hand. She hesitated and seemed annoyed as she prompted me,

"Go ahead, Theodore, you may answer."

I was delighted to have been chosen to answer yet again.

I stood up, stretched my arm upwards eagerly and blurted out the answer, then she dropped her bomb shell on my little toes,

"Theodore," She said in a calm loud voice,

"Theodore . . . you have to stop answering in Greek, you must speak English."

The whole class laughed at me, I sat down, one deflated and confused little boy.

English, off course! What a fool I had been if only I had been prepared.

For me the first playground break did not come soon enough, I was pleased to be outside and even more pleased to see my big sister Androulla walk up to me with two of her friends.

After my brief hysterical outburst on how I had embarrassed myself, Androulla nodded in her usual cool headed manner she told me that I should relax, that was how school was. She gave me the confidence to give this school thing one more try.

*   *   *

1963, London

Now here is the next problem, one huge problem.

After months of school, things seemed to be moving in the right direction until one morning, whilst we were in morning registration. The class room door opened and in he walked,

Abdul Kadir.

Most of the names in this book have been changed to protect the innocent, but Abdul Kadir's name has not been altered in the hope that he will be named and shamed.

Our teacher announced his arrival.

"Class, we have a new pupil joining us to-day, he is from Pakistan and his name is Abdul, Abdul Kadir."

From where I was sitting, I could see that all the children were staring at this one individual boy,

I remember watching each pupil's lower lip drop.

They were in awe as they like me, stared at Abdul Kadir.

He was taller in height than our teacher.

Abdul must have been over five feet tall and I really wanted to say,

'This must be the wrong class for this giant, I might only be five years old, but hey lady , I and the rest are not so stupid this does not feel right, get him out of here.'

Even now until this day I have yet to meet a five year old boy as tall as Abdul Kadir.

Perhaps there were other reasons for him joining our class, was he really just a five year old in the body of a fifteen year old?

Well strange things did seem to happen during the sixties.

Thankfully Abdul was not made to sit near me but I did notice that the boy and the girl he had been placed between were looking pretty worried as Abdul sat uncomfortably on the small wooden chair that was much too small for him.

During the next playground break, I spotted Abdul Kadir.

Four other boys from our class were with him.

I figured that his intimidating size must have inspired them to befriend him and quickly . . . just in case he found a reason to dislike them.

For me, things only got worse.

I noticed his four followers laughing and cajoling and urging Abdul on inspiring him and pointing him in a specific direction . . . towards me!

I stood with my back against the brick wall as they approached; one of them who was named Timmy shouted with bravado,

"Abdul wants to try a trick on you Theodore." The other three boys giggled.

"No thanks." I replied sheepishly.

"You do not have a choice." Howard warned as young Derek stuck his little freckled face in front of mine and squeaked,

"If you don't let him do it, we will have to hold you down Theodore."

I was truly petrified.

"Alright but it is just a joke though isn't it?" I pleaded, trying to be brave and I do recall that I was crying.

They sniggered as they moved aside creating a gap for their leader and then . . . Abdul Kadir walked up to me, so close that our toes were touching.

He stared down at me, he had the biggest set of teeth I had ever seen as he flashed his evil smile and then without warning reached out with his right hand, placed it on my shoulder and using his thumb and index finger squeezed my little school pullover while he pinched as much of my shoulder skin together as he could gather and then violently twisted my skin.

I screamed from the intense agony, the sudden pain forced me to drop to my knees.

The Abdul Kadir gang ran off across the playground, looking very pleased with their newly found torture as I tried to rub the hurt from my shoulder.

From that day on the torturous grip I nicknamed as 'an Abdul Kadir' was born.

(Sorry to my kids . . . but I only did the Abdul Kadir gently on you)

On the way home my sister succeeded in cheering me up by telling me of the wonderful delight that awaited us that weekend, a trip to Battersea fun fair in Battersea Park. I loved the fair and the exciting rides there.

Then she sang, she would often sing and I think I sometimes sang along with her.

We both liked the catchy Helen Shapiro song, *Walking Back to Happiness* and on that day it seemed quite appropriate.

After a few minutes we reached the sweet shop at the top of Barcombe Avenue and my sister bought for me a liquorice sherbet dip, it tasted so nice that all the nastiness of the day quickly receded into some far flung corner of my little brain.

We were never given front door keys to our house when we were children as there was always somebody at home to open the door. So I ran ahead of my sister and rapped the brass knocker a few times, I was looking forward to seeing my mum, so that I could tell her about the nasty and evil Abdul Kadir.

Through the frosted glass I saw her moving towards me. The door swung open and my little mouth fell open as I looked up at her.

Not my mother.

She was the same height and the same build, but definitely a different person.

My sister had caught up with me and we stood next to each other and stared at the stranger who had just opened the door.

She was pretty with dark hair and quite a lot younger than our mother but the most awful thing about her was the fact that she was smiling at us, even though she had a large black eye patch over her left eye. Was she a pirate?

"Hello." She said.

"My Name is May, I am the new lodger."

London 1964

 May had enrolled as a second year student learning Architecture at a London University and it only took us a few hours to warm to her friendly and kind demeanour.

She lived in the small converted attic room on the top floor of our house and although she would always find time to play games with us there were many lengthy periods when she would retreat to her room to study or perhaps just to find solitude with herself.

  One September day a loud banging on our front door awoke me and everyone else in the house.

 It was three in the morning and the hammering on the door did not stop until my father went down the stairs and opened the door.

 My sister and I watched from the top of the stairs.

The person who had invaded our privacy was Nick the Greek.

 He walked into the hall way and my father ushered him into the front dining room as he called up to us to 'go back to bed'.

Muffled anguished cries from Nick the Greek filtered up through the house as we strained our ears to listen in vain for any clues that would help us to understand what might have prompted such an untimely emergency.

In the morning it was decided that my sister would not be attending school, she had not slept well because of the furore in the early hours and even though I also made a case for fatigue, I was told to go to school on my own.

It was a beautiful sunny morning and under my arm I carried a special gift my mother had purchased for me from a toy store in Brixton market, a three quarter length cricket set with a soft ball and three light sticks for a wicket.

They were brand spanking new and very authentic looking. I loved them.

Dinner hour came and I ate quickly, which I should confirm is quite normal for me during any meal time.

After I ate my school lunch I ventured out into the playground with my bat and ball and to my delight several other children accepted my invitation to play cricket.

We used the west facing brick wall to lean the wicket against and we began to play.

I was inspired, I bowled three batsmen out and then it was my turn to bat. I held my bat in front of me as if I was a real cricket player and I was ready for the first ball.

I looked down at my chalk line crease and looked back up.

My vision was obscured by a shadow because . . . standing in my line of batting and staring down at me was Abdul Kadir. What was he doing? Did he want to bat?

No.

He snatched my wonderful cricket bat from my hands and threw it across the concrete playground, the bat bounced several times finally stopping flat side down.

I feared the worst as I ran towards the bat, it was broken but perhaps still useable, I picked it up and ran back to my friends to continue our game.

They had all gone. Abdul Kadir had frightened them all away.

At the end of school I walked to the school exit prepared to walk home alone but surprisingly May was standing near the gate waiting for me.

She smiled and put her arm on my shoulder. May spotted the tears in my eyes.

May stooped down and asked me why I was so unhappy. So I told her about the playground incident.

This was not the first time I had told May about the monster that was Abdul Kadir.

She stood up and looked into the school playground as I tugged at her arm,

"Come on May, let's go home." I said.

May turned to me and said,

"Stay here, do not move, I will be back shortly do you understand what I am telling you?"

There was a real venomous tone to her voice. It worried me. This was a fired up May I did not know.

"Yes." I said quietly as I watched her stride purposefully across the playground towards Abdul Kadir and his gang.

She looked back towards me as she neared them and pointed at the gang of boys, she shouted out so that everyone could hear,

"Is this him?"

I nodded and I stepped inside the school entrance so that I could see more clearly.

I saw May walk into the midst of the gang and jab her finger at Abdul Kadir's face. He tried to appear unaffected by May's threatening behaviour, but within seconds he looked very worried.

One of the boys, Timmy tried to escape but May grabbed his arm and yanked him back into the group.

They were facing her . . . all five of them but I still couldn't hear May's voice although her finger was jabbing at them like a deadly dagger.

They all seemed very sad and frightened I had never seen them looking so miserable and I was beginning to worry about any retribution and revenge attacks after this confrontation, it would surely seal my fate I felt doomed but then it happened.

My curiosity forced me to take a few more steps towards the unfolding incident.

First it was Timmy who bent over double and threw up.

Then the other three boys lowered their heads as they began to puke.

Amongst them all Abdul kadir stood still and alone there was an incredible look of fear and panic across his face as May leant forward, so close that she almost touched his face with her nose.

Slowly and deliberately as if in slow motion May pulled the eye patch away from her head until her bad eye socket was exposed and unprotected.

She stared with her good eye at him as she moved her dead eye into Abdul Kadir's immediate line of vision.

I heard his deep muffled scream bellow out and reverberate across the playground and out into the street, it reminded me of a killer whale's last cry.

Yet to me it sounded more gratifying than listening to a classical symphony. It gave me a satisfied feeling and I was still smiling as May called me over to where she stood with the frightened gang of boys.

She placed her eye patch back over her bad eye and she shoved me in front of them. With her hands on my shoulders she warned them,

"This is my Theodore and I am here to tell you again, never forget what I told you and keep away from him . . . or next time I will do the same, but a hundred times worse and I will come to your houses and I will do it in front of your families and when they ask me why I am doing this, you will have to tell them the reason why."

We walked away from them as the headmistress followed by two teachers ran past us towards the five boys.

We were out of the gates and homeward bound before anyone could question us.

"What did you say to them?" I asked her.

May smiled and patted my head "Nothing of any importance." She said.

*   *   *

During the later months of 1964 I am sure I was not alone in being afraid of all varieties of bird that were flying in the sky or more dangerously sitting on a roof top staring down at me, I had seen the advertising clips for the year's top film by Mister Hitchcock and like many other children of my age I understood only too well that the pigeon sitting up there warbling away could be a lookout for the other million or so birds waiting to swoop down to savage me and in particular peck the eyes out of my head just like the graphic scenes in the advertising posters.

I was home alone as mum was visiting relatives who lived three doors along.

For me, lying on the floor reading a super hero comic was as good as it got and it was while I was staring at a full page graphic advert of the film; **The Birds** that I was startled by an impatient loud knocking on the front door.

I opened the door.

Nick the Greek stood in the doorway.

His large body took up all the door space and as always we had nothing to say to each other.

He looked down at my inquisitive expression as I stared at his sweaty fat face. He bore several scratch marks on his cheeks and forehead, some of the cuts were still bleeding and I assumed that the horror film birds must have swooped down and attacked him.

Nick pushed me aside and barged into the house.

I looked outside, searching for killer birds.

"George, George," He shouted as he ran through the house and then ran back towards me.

"Where is he?" He shouted.

I did not speak.

"Where is your father, you little shit?"

I shrugged my shoulders.

Nick looked as if he wanted to inflict injury upon me.

I held my breath as he finally reached a decision and decided to leave.

It was a relief to see him walk out of the house. I began to close the door.

Nick stopped abruptly with his back towards me as if he had forgotten something.

He turned around, pushed the door open and stood towering above me.

I looked at his large face as he said,

"Tell your dad I was here looking for him."

I did not speak nor did I expect Nick to raise his hand and slap me heavily across the cheek.

The slap left my cheek throbbing, but I refused to cry as he sneered, turned on his heels and walked hurriedly away.

Barcombe Avenue was quite a long road and as Nick the Greek turned aggressively away from our house he collided with my uncle Spiros who was in turn carrying out his happy daily ritual of cutting a single baby rose from the bush in our front garden and inserting it in his lapel buttonhole.

Nick the Greek cursed at Spiros and even though he was several inches shorter than Nick. The smartly dressed Spiros retaliated with an effective slick verbal attack which forced Nick to shut up and walk away.

That evening while watching television I took particular interest in a TV programme called: **Police Five**.

I suppose it was the first of its kind, a predecessor equivalent to to-days **Crime Watch UK** in which real unsolved crimes are reported in the hope of prompting valuable witnesses from the watching public to come forward.

I watched in vain, hoping that at least one of the photo-fit pictures of suspected criminals would match the description of Nick the Greek, which might in turn result in his arrest and prosecution.

A terrible thing happened the following Sunday.

*   *   *

It was one of my father's customs that when there were no weddings or other celebrations to attend on a Sunday, my father and mother and my sister and I would go along with at least two uncles and aunts to Catford dog Stadium in South East London.

The stadium was an arena with plenty of seating banks that surrounded an oval race track. Up to eight Greyhounds would race against each other by chasing an electric hare that ran anti – clockwise around the outside edge of the track.

When we got there we sat in the glass enclosure and before the first race we were, to my horror joined at our table by Nick the Greek.

He spoke briefly with my father George and promptly left our enclosure.

During the following few minute's intense secretive discussions took place between my father and my uncles George and Chris. The only thing I managed to learn after straining to hear their conversation was: Six, the number six. Which I presumed somehow related to the number six greyhound in one of the forthcoming greyhound races.

So we watched the first race.

All I could hear from my father and my uncles were cries of encouragement for the number six dog,

"Come on six."

We went through nine of the ten races and none of them were won by the number six dog.

By this time my father and my uncles looked very down and miserable.

Yet just before the last race was run my father and uncles produced large wads of cash and one of them took the money and went up to a betting window, eventually returning with a large wad of freshly struck tickets.

There must have been at least fifty tickets each marked with the words 'Five pounds - win - Trap Six, race Ten'

This was pretty exciting; even I understood that all the money had been laid on trap six and that it had to win in order for them to collect their winnings.

So the electric hare whirred and bobbled around the track and as it passed the trap containing the dogs; the trap lids pinged open and the dogs hurtled out onto the sandy track in pursuit of the bunny.

I watched the race unfold amidst many cries of encouragement.

The number six dog led to the first bend and then into the straight section for the first time, we cheered as the number six dog went further ahead around the second bend . . . but . . . another greyhound; the number one dog came around the inside bend with a really fast run and as the dogs negotiated the bend the one dog barged sideways against the six dog there were gasps of disappointment as the six dog was effectively knocked off its legs and out of the race.

I looked up at my father and my uncles but their attention was still focused on the dog track so I looked back at the track and saw that the racing dogs were approaching the finish line.

That is when it happened.

There was something else on the track, not just the electric hare and the greyhounds - there was a large moving object in the middle of the track running head on towards the greyhounds.

It was Nick the Greek.

Everyone in the stadium stood to their feet jeering and complaining as stadium security staff began to clamber over the barriers to get onto the track.

Nick the Greek had already turned and was fleeing down the middle of the track chased by a posse of staff and . . . the dogs.

For a man of his size he moved really quickly, his shirt tail was flapping around the outside of his trousers as his elbows swung furiously in an effort to make him run faster. Nick almost fell from the track as he half jumped a section of the fence before making his escape across a deserted seating section.

So (I guess that was the plan all along) the race was deemed as void and everyone who had bet on it got their money back.

The next morning on my way to school I stopped at a telephone booth went inside it and from my school duffle bag took a strip of paper on which I had written a telephone number.

I placed a three penny bit into the coin slot and dialled the advertised number for 'Police Five'

A woman answered and asked me how she could help? I told her in a hushed voice.

"The man who ran onto the racetrack at Catford stadium yesterday was Nick the Greek."

There was a pause before she replied.

"I see and would you know his second name please caller?"

"No." I whispered

"So what is your name?"

I replaced the phone back on the hook.

Perhaps I would wait for justice to catch up with Nick the Greek in some other way, for now at least.

*   *   *

1964

The remainder of   Nineteen sixty four was a crazy year in our house, in the first respect; it was full of people.

My mum's sister's Dimitra and Hariklou along with her husband Christofi had arrived from Cyprus.

To add to that my father's cousin Zacharias had also arrived.

May the lodger was still living with us and then to top it all - my mother's younger brother Chris had also decided to come and live with us.

My sister Androulla and I welcomed the friendly company and we both giggled at the names because everyone called Zacharias; Sugar which was the literal meaning of his name and everyone called Christofi; Toffee.

For some weird reason Barcombe Avenue had become densely populated with Greeks - the Cypriot variety.

Across the road lived my dad's sister Andrika and her husband George with their boys John, Nick and Andrew.

Further up the road lived uncle Spiros and auntie Elleni with their children Michael, Doulla and Stella and further down the road were Uncle Chris and auntie Aredi with their children Charlie, Maria and Georgina.

I need to stop here because there were at least seven more Greek families within walking distance of our house.

More often than not after school - my sister and I were allowed to play out on the street with our many cousins.

We would stay out there in the warm sunshine until the sun set. Happy days although I guess our little group must have irritated some of the neighbours.

It must be said that as first/second generation immigrants we were never intimidated or upset by English customs in fact we were impressed by them and strived to adapt and ease into the wonderful English way of life and today we can honestly say that we are proud to be so lovingly accepted here and off course our children are much more English than us although each and every one of them is extremely proud of their Greek Cypriot heritage.

During the sixties school summer holidays were halcyon days and it was during that time that one certain young Greek couple would walk very quickly down Barcombe Avenue. Georgie and Irene were their names and they were so obviously madly in love with each other - well that's the impression we got and even though we were very young they afforded us a tiny part of their precious time by always saying hello.

Every single time they walked past us we would all stop and stare at them.

It was because of their sudden appearance from over the hill; they looked like they were always in a terrible hurry.

Georgie, who I must say would nowadays be considered a doppelganger for the Hollywood actor *Ben Stiller* was always grinning, why he smiled so much I remember once having the time to count his teeth as he approached us and Irene's cheeks were always blushing.

As they rushed past us they always held each other's hands tightly, I imagined that Georgie was afraid to let go of her in case she was swallowed up by some mysterious black hole or perhaps they liked the current Beatle's hit; *I want To Hold Your Hand.*

They were always in a rush as little Irene who wore high heeled shoes would move her skinny little legs as fast as she could in an effort to keep up with Georgie.

I had never seen such a happy couple and it often made me wonder that perhaps these two happy young people had not been party to an arranged Greek Marriage, the wedding dating game that Greek Cypriots call; Broxenia.

Or maybe they were?

I had overheard my mother and her sisters on many occasions suggesting that various young eligible single people they knew should be matched together with each other and I had also seen some of their recommendations come to fruition.

I suppose they were brain washed from their early years in Cyprus as such matters over there were common place - a habit which must have been hard to shrug off.

*   *   *

Cyprus 1948

EOKA was the name of the Greek movement in Cyprus that wanted Nationalism.

They were recognised as a political movement in 1955, classed as anti - British Empire and anti the Turkish resistance organisation.

Several people got swept up in the fervour of Nationalism.

The usual reasons of different religions and different cultures were key in fuelling rivalry and dislike between Greek and Turkish Cypriots.

The young men of Cyprus were swept along by the fervour of their peers.

I would like to believe that testosterone is the main driving force behind all young men of that age and during those troubled days although George was not a member of EOKA he had more than his fair share of drive and determination that spurred him on in that ultimate objective, to put the island of Cyprus under the complete control of Greece.

They marched and demonstrated with the EOKA flag intimidating the Turkish people and off course the Turkish resistance movement retaliated.

One hot August day George with his father Philipos rode on the back of their mules from their village of Yialousa in Northern Cyprus heading towards a market town in order to sell their reserve stocks of lambs and Goats.

Directly in their path was the nearby Turkish Village of Vokolida and in those troubled days sensible Greeks steered clear of passing through Turkish villages and vice versa.

But not George and his father Philipos, they were both stubborn and fearless.

Philipos was a tall thin man who was well known for his no nonsense approach to life.

A hard peasant upbringing on the relatively poor island of Cyprus had hardened his outlook on life so much so that friends and family accepted him for the hard hitting intense out - spoken person he had become.

They rode slowly onto the deserted dusty white hill roads of Vokolida village.

The only noises that could be heard came from some squawking chickens in a nearby house as they continued along the unkempt winding dirt track.

"Where are the villagers?" George asked.

Philipos smiled.

"They are wary of us, just wait, you will see them shortly." He said.

Philipos guessed right.

As the bend in the road unwound their route was blocked by several Turks.

The Greeks had no option but to stop.

"You are blocking the path." Philipos shouted at them.

"You have no right to come through our village" Warned one of the Turkish men who had a rifle slung over his shoulder.

"Move out of our way, we are only passing through." Philipos argued.

Another Turkish man, tall and wide shouldered walked up to them.

"Who do you think you are? Do you not understand what we could do to you?"

"Yes and do you think you would have it all your own way?" Philipos replied.

Four men advanced towards them as back up for their fellow Turk.

The wide shouldered man nodded negatively. He spoke slowly and with passion,

"This is the trouble my friend, you are Greek and we are Turkish, we have the right to defend our village and you have no right to impose yourselves on us, now turn around and go back another way, do you hear me?"

A young Turkish boy threw a stone which struck George's mule.

George quickly dismounted ready to retaliate against the boy.

"George, come back here now." Philipos barked.

The wide shouldered Turkish man shouted angrily at his own son.

Philipos gestured to the Turk.

"You see, you attacked us first."

The Turks glared at Philipos.

"Tell you what. " Philipos suggested,

"Let your boy fight mine, if your boy wins we will turn around and go back. If my boy beats yours then we will continue, what say you?"

The Turks liked the idea, they made agreeable comments and the wide shouldered man nodded.

"Very well, my boy Arif will punish you by inflicting pain on your little bastard, let them fight."

Philipos nodded to George and then warned him,

"Do not lose."

The Turkish lad Arif and George ran at one another, they punched and kicked each other as the Turks cheered their boy on.

Philipos watched in silence.

George fell and landed on his back.

Arif launched himself into the air in an attempt to stamp on George's head.

The only thing George was able to do was to lift his right leg vertically and as Arif landed he caught the full impact of George's foot in his lower parts.

Arif screamed as he dropped to his knees and doubled over in agony.

His father stared at Philipos,

"Take your son and get out of our village,"

Philipos beckoned to George to re-mount the mule and they prepared to move forward.

"Listen to me Greek." The Turkish man warned.

"Never come through here again. If you do we will kill you, do you understand?"

Philipos nodded.

"I understand." He replied.

They rode past the Turkish people as the little Turkish boy sat up and found his breath he stared up at George menacingly.

At the top of the road George looked back to see that the Turkish boy was still glaring at him.

*   *   *

London 1952.

In those early post war years if you came from a little place like Cyprus to a huge city like London you were bound to be overwhelmed.

Seventeen year old George was impressed by the bright city lights and the excitement of London Town.

He stood in the reception hall of the glitzy Piccadilly Hotel in central London waiting for the chief of staff Mr Loizou to respond to his request for a job interview, the contact that had been given to him by one of his relatives in Gloucester.

George stood facing the pretty Piccadilly Hotel receptionist with the Lana Turner hair style as she smiled back at him.

"Mr Loizou has asked for you to take a seat, he won't be long."

"Thank you." George said in his most polite voice.

"But if you don't mind I will stand here." She smiled at him some more.

A voice broke through the pleasantries as mister Loizou approached.

"George? Is that you?"

George nodded.

"Yes Sir."

"Where did you get my name from George?"

"My cousin Andreas in Gloucester Sir, he said you were a good friend of his."

"Andreas?"

"Andreas Paschalis Sir" George replied.

Mr Loizou smiled.

"Andreas worked for me a long time ago, how is he?"

"He is very well sir."

"Okay George you had best come with me for an interview, follow me."

"Yes sir."

"George, please do not call me sir, mister Loizou will be fine."

"Yes sir mister Loizou."

In the staff quarters several waiters and waitresses were busy moving laundry and silver cutlery, a few of them looked at him inquisitively.

The interview was concluded successfully and Mister Loizou shook George's hand.

"When are you able to start?"

"I can start now mister Loizou."

"Okay good, I'll get one of the other staff to show you around for the first couple of days, help you acclimatise."

Mr Loizou called one of the head waiters over.

"Johnny, come over here, this is George, he is starting work with us to-day, take him with you and just let him tag along and help out for now."

Johnny showed George around and eventually he asked George to help another waiter prepare the dining tables in one of the function rooms.

Johnny asked George to put the table clothes and silver cutlery on the banqueting tables.

The other waiter a tall darker skinned young man was busy opening up the tables by unfolding the legs and standing them in readiness for the adornment of the silver service equipment when he caught sight of George's face.

George was too busy with his duties to notice that the other waiter was walking menacingly towards him.

Just at the last second George sensed an impending danger, he noticed that the man who was walking towards him did not appear to be in good humour he looked to be irritated and irked by something.

"What is the matter" George asked staring at the olive skinned man who was in the process of raising an arm.

The man punched George squarely on the nose and knocked him to the ground.

A terrible fight ensued and the function room's tables were knocked aside as the two men fought.

The noise attracted Johnny and mister Loizou who ran into the room and pulled the two men apart.

"What the hell is going on here George, you have not even been here one hour?"

"And you Arif, why have you done this."

George looked at the other man, Arif,

"You are Arif . . . the Turkish boy from Cyprus, now I remember you."

"Enough. Both of you come to my office now."

George explained to Mister Loizou about the past events that had taken place in Cyprus.

Arif was questioned and was then honest enough to admit the truth - he was dismissed instantly.

George remained in employment at the Piccadilly hotel for a further two years.

*   *   *

1964

There we were again, walking through Atlantic Road Brixton, we negotiated a path through the Saturday Shoppers, it was the best day of the week for me, because there was only one place I wanted to visit amongst the market stalls of Brixton, the second hand comic's stall on Atlantic Road.

 From the age of five, I had visited that street stall most Saturdays and had insisted that my mother Effie and sister Androulla waited while I selected my three or four comics from the hundreds that were available, I only opted for Superman and Batman Comics, the cost was sixpence each.

You have to believe me when I tell you that I had accumulated a huge collection that started from the number one editions up to the three hundreds.

 Even then, I felt that I had achieved a great deal by sifting through various comics every week to find back numbers that I could add to my collection.

 On paper now, I can honestly say that at the age of ten I was a multi -millionaire thanks to the current value of my comics.

Then it was on to mother's favourite shop, the Greek Delicatessen in Electric Avenue.

It was a busy little store, you could have got from one side to the other in three strides and it was crammed with scores of meats and hanging strings of aromatic spicy Loukanika pork sausages. The strong pungent smell of coriander merged with the aroma of other imported vegetables, newly baked Greek sesame seeded bread and freshly ground Turkish coffee, nothing else compares.

One Saturday as my mother and sister waited for me to select my comics from Brixton market my mother decided that she had to go and buy her Greek stuff and advised me to stay put.

"Stay here at this stall and I will return shortly." She ordered.

That was fine by me.

As I flicked through the back editions, the owner of the stall asked me a question,

"Listen here sonny, you bought a Superman DC number three a couple of weeks ago, do you remember?"

"Yes." I answered.

"Well how about bringing it back to me next week and I will let you pick any ten comics you want as an exchange?"

I did not even give the suggestion the slightest consideration.

As I carried on searching the back numbers I said,

"No thank you"

The stall owner seemed annoyed and looked at another man that was standing beside him. He said to the man,

"Sorry Frank"

Frank, a ginger haired man with loads of freckles leant down and placed his face so near to mine that I could smell his nicotine breath, I felt intimidated.

"Listen son, I need that comic, now name your price."

That was enough to frighten me.

I walked away from them and ran straight to the Greek Deli where my mother and sister were still waiting to be served.

To get back home we had to wait for a red - double decker bus at a bus stop queue on the A23 which at the time, seemed like the biggest bus stop queue in the world.

It was on the Brixton road in between the new underground station and Coldharbour Lane and we would sometimes wait for three or four buses to come along before finding room to board.

When we finally boarded, the bus conductor would announce,

"All aboard, hold tight"

How good was that.

Well on that day when we finally reached our home bus stop, we had been told by the conductor to sit on the top floor of the bus and as we trundled down the stairs I spotted Frank the ginger haired man from the market stall standing in the bus aisle.

We got off the bus and as it moved away I stared in vain through the window to get another look at the Ginger haired man.

We walked up the hill and back to our house, it was a warm sunny day and my sister suggested that we should visit the little park at the top of our road.

I loved the play area there so we knocked on some doors and we gathered our cousins together, about ten of us walked up to Hillside Park.

My mother told us that if she was not at home when we returned she would be at Aredi's house down the road.

We must have spent three hours playing there and finally we began our walk home.

When we reached our front door I spotted the Ginger man, Frank.

It seemed that he had just left our house and he was struggling to carry a heavy old suitcase.

I realised that this dodgy looking character could have been inside our house and that he had quite possibly stolen my comics.

What should I do?

Georgie and Irene were walking up the road.

Frank was walking down it.

They were on a collision course, would Georgie and Irene let go of each other's hand and allow Frank to pass?

I called out to Georgie and Irene who as usual were in their own sweet loved up world.

"Stop him, that man has stolen my comics"

Georgie's facial expression was confused. Irene's smile vanished.

"Hey, look here" Georgie shouted at the ginger haired man.

They came within inches of each other and Frank pushed through Georgie and Irene's human link so violently that Irene fell off her high heels.

As Georgie helped her back up Frank made his escape, with my never to be found again fortune.

*   *   *

Here's the selfish and terribly guilty bit.

As young boy brought up with home grown values and allowed to play on the pavements of a Streatham residential street you - as did all the other Greek children – you get drawn in to a culture that gives you your first impressions of belonging to a group.

All the kids on Barcombe Avenue were lovely adorable children.

Up the road on the left lived a school pal Brian; he was six years of age, the same as me and we were both in the same class at school.

One day Brian's mum suggested that I visit their house and play. So my mum was very grateful and I was allowed to visit Brian's house.

In his extended loft he had the most amazing train set laid out across the whole boarded out floor – there were model platforms – vintage steam trains – level crossings and miniature passengers and just about everything you would find on a railway system. It was fantastic and Brian was such a nice kid, I appreciated the visit and will never forget their kindness.

One lovely summer's eve during the school holidays I was playing with my cousins outside John, Nick and Andrew's house when I spotted something . . . a group of children who were laughing and chatting were advancing down the road towards us.

I quickly realised that they were heading straight for our group and that we would have to mingle as they passed through.

Because I was (and still am) pretty impulsive and stupid I took it upon myself to become the protector of our little gang. Why?

Right up until this day I do not know, there is no logical reason as to why a six year old would do something so rash - but I did.

I picked up a tiny crab apple and threw it at the approaching children. It was my warning shot.

 'Get back or cross the road . . . keep away from us'

The crab apple struck little Brian in his left eye. Blood spurted from his wound as Brian screamed and ran home to his mummy. I ran home and hid in the downstairs toilet and after a while heard the door knock and the voices of Brian's mother and mine discussing what I had done.

It must have been very traumatic for Brian and if you ever get to read this Brian . . . please accept my sincere apology it was the first time I had ever thrown anything at any one and the last.

In the years that followed I made many life changing decisions and even on a massive industrial scale such as maintaining and controlling Streatham Ice Rink – which was often fraught with danger . . . nothing I have ever done is as bad as my stupid crab apple direct hit on poor young Brian.

Sorry Brian.

*   *   *   *

1969

The Great Hall - Epsom district Hospital. Surrey

This is what it feels like . . . the very first time you do it.

There are nine hundred people seated around the auditorium, you are thirteen years of age and you are the focus of all their attention. All those people are staring straight at you and believe me . . . you do not want to be there.

 Your trainer pushes your elbow and nudges you up three steps that you would rather not climb.

You really do not want to go through with this.

 The bright white canvas reflecting the powerful spotlights dazzle your eyes.

Then you lift your legs over the ropes and enter the arena.

You are on your own.

 It is true what they say that there is no salvation at that precise moment.

 The knot in your stomach twists and tightens – it is a unique feeling.

A man in a black tuxedo walks into the boxing ring with a microphone and announces you to the crowd, they applaud you and then they applaud your opponent who is standing on the opposite side of the boxing arena.

 For him also . . . it is his first ever fight.

My sister and my mum and dad and my little brother are sitting in the front row.

But I can't hear their cries of encouragement all I hear is a garbled noise.

I look across at my opponent.

He is a bit shorter than me and he also looks as if he is about to burst into tears.

The big fat man wearing a white shirt who is called the referee hooks a finger at us both; the signal that orders us to meet in the middle and 'touch gloves' out of respect for Queensberry rules.

We go back to our designated corners and stand there, waiting.

The crowd's noise stops abruptly.

Someone sitting at a table nearby rings a great big bell that signals the start of the boxing contest and you think,

'Oh my goodness, what am I doing here? '

The baying spectators urge you on.

You force your legs forward and keep those nice big soft gloves held up high in front of your face for protection.

Fear is your only companion, motivating you in more ways than any pep talk could ever do.

You throw a punch that hits the air again and again, jab, jab, jab, until, contact is made.

The nerves and fear evaporate from that point because all your emotions and senses are now fully employed by the part of the brain that is trying to solve the puzzle of finding a way through your opponent's defences.

I never wanted to be a boxer but my father George insisted that it would be good for me and so after months of training there I was, still pretty useless and unprepared for this my first amateur boxing bout.

That evening at eight pm. the time my first bout started I could have been at home watching the 1969 Miss World Contest on live TV!

What a bummer.

I won that fight purely because my reach was three inches longer than my opponents and through sheer panic and fear I jabbed out my fists as quickly and as fast as I could. The other lad could not get near me. My hand was held aloft; little me the boy in the Red corner from Wandsworth ABA was the winner.

So I had a short boxing career and almost by default was fortunate enough to go on and become the London Schoolboy lightweight junior Champion even though I was truly awful at the sport of boxing.

Strange how things have a way of coming back around full circle.

* * *

1977

The Great Ballroom

The Grosvenor House Hotel. Park Lane. London

The finest cutlery and the finest linen adorned the huge circular banqueting tables. Seated around the tables were hundreds of A class celebrities as well as the world's leading sportsmen and sports women.

I was there too.

All of the guests had been invited by the organisers of the Miss World Competition; *Eric and Julia Morley* to partake in the lavish post dinner and dance celebrations of the evening's earlier live televised ceremony known as the *Miss World* competition.

That afternoon I had received an unexpected telephone call from the General Manager of Streatham Ice Rink, Brian Bowman who had asked me to get myself over to Park Lane for the evening function so that I could act as one of the security staff in the great ballroom.

So there I stood just in front of the kitchen swing doors. Guarding the fire exits in case any members of the press should find a way in and if they did I was to escort them back out again.

At the time I was an assistant manager at Streatham Ice Rink and as part of the MECCA organisation we were often called upon to help out with other company interests, *Miss World* being one of them.

For the first hour I took my duties very seriously and guarded the exit doors with impeccable attention. I did eventually realise that no one could possibly get inside the ballroom without coming through the main entrance so I went on a walk - about.

As I was dressed in a black evening suit none of the guests realised that I was just a lowly paid member of staff.

After their three course meal, the guests began to mingle.

It became easy for me to blend in amongst them.

The oddity that I walked past immediately grabbed my attention, so I stopped and stared.

A long queue of elderly men had formed.

I counted thirty five dinner suited gents in that line.

The other notion that struck me was that these guys looked happy to be waiting in a queue.

It defied logic, why be happy when you are made to wait?

The reason was standing at the front of the queue.

Greeting and smiling at the men as they took their turn to congratulate her was *Mary Stavin* the twenty year old winner of the beauty pageant.

What else could I do?

I had to get in line.

When I eventually got to the front of the queue Mary gave me the most wonderful smile, she was probably pleased to finally be congratulated by someone her own age and we exchanged a little peck on the cheek as we held hands in a hand shake perhaps we were taking too long because a voice from behind me called out,

"Come on mate, get a move on"

Sadly I turned away from Mary and then I spotted the man who had told me to 'move on' it was the famous Manchester United footballer *George Best*.

*   *   *

From an early age, Streatham Ice rink had become my one and only haunt.

Like so many people I was hooked on its amazing attraction which had offered so much for all its patrons.

It was a Universe in itself, like a Sun pulling around the worlds of the Ice Hockey Clubs and the Ice Speed skaters and the figure skaters and not forgetting the social skaters.

Each and every organisation fitted snuggly into a niche doing their thing yet somehow managing to act together as one.

I used to compare it to a huge ship every time I visited the engine room with the chief engineer John Osment. It never ceased to impress upon me how so much effort, preparation and machinery went into maintaining that one single slab of ice that everyone wanted to glide across.

Halloween night 1978

There were two thousand seven hundred people inside our ice rink, it was a Saturday evening and disc jockey Memphis was swinging his shoulders on stage while playing one of the year's top hits; *Rivers Of Babylon* by *Boney M.*

Engineers John and Gary had rigged up a surprise Halloween trick which would be revealed on the stroke of midnight. It was hard to see any of the ice due to the large volume of skaters using up all the skating area.

Down in the skate hire, the six young lads were doing their best to serve the long queues of people waiting to hire a pair of the ice rinks own supply of ice skates.

I helped out for a bit trying to inspire the boys to work as quickly as possible.

Noticeably my young cousin Nick to whom I had given a skate hire job had once again sneaked away to be with his latest girlfriend and it took me a few minutes to hunt him down and drag him back into the skate hire.

Nights like those were great fun but hectic, so I was relieved to see the queues diminish as all the skaters were eventually kitted out with skates and on the ice.

I liked to walk around the balcony of the ice rink looking down at the throng of people skating anti clock wise and from up there you could always spot a minor fight or accident.

I went down to the stage and spoke to Memphis,

"Is everything prepared for midnight?" I asked him.

Memphis as always looked at me side - ways, he had a habit of doing that.

"Hope so, you had better speak to John and Gary, I don't want to be responsible for any accidents" He shouted above the music in his Brummie accent.

"What do you mean by that?" I asked.

"You'll see" He said and went back to his turn tables. I walked away from the stage.

Memphis always liked to err on the side of caution.

At the stroke of midnight, the lights were turned off, the whole ice rink fell into darkness, I was not liking it one bit, I found myself running over to the stage hoping to tell Memphis to make an announcement that everyone should stop skating and stand completely still, immediately.

Thankfully he had the common sense to do just that before I reached him and any accidents were avoided as, through the absolute blackness a huge silver fireball high in the ceiling lit up one corner of the ice rink.

The sound of cackling and howling witches exploded through the powerful speakers as people began to scream in anticipation.

On the corner of the area that the fireball had erupted from, a large spotlight operated by Gary picked out the source of the flare a huge figure of a wicked witch all dressed in black, pointed hat and all was on a witches broom flying along a thin cable which went across the entire length of the ice rink and as the silver firework under the broom propelled the witch forwards, the whole thing dipped lower and lower, heading for the skaters.

"Watch out" Memphis warned in vain.

The burning witch fell on the ice, missing skaters by inches.

The lights came back on and thankfully a serious accident was avoided.

The session finished and as the building gradually emptied, the speed skaters arrived for a late night training session, speed skate official Lynn as usual was in good humour,

"Any chance of a couple more of those witches being lit just behind my lot please Theo, it might make them go a bit faster" she joked.

John walked over to me sporting his usual calm demeanour,

"That went okay then" He said calmly.

"Don't think we'll try that again somehow John, do you?" I said.

"Perhaps not" He laughed.

*   *   *

Halloween Night Streatham Ice Rink 1974

The queue to enter the ice rink snaked all the way around the building. The doors were about to open and allow the mainly teenage crowd to enter.

Hidden in amongst the skaters were thirty bad boys with no intention of entering the building.

They were there to carry out a savage attack.

Under their long raincoats they carried concealed weapons, knives, metal bars and swords. The bad boys were only intent on one thing.

Little Chris was part of our group, we did not realise at the time that the only reason he was so short in height was because he'd lied about his age he was in fact just thirteen years old instead of the seventeen years he claimed to be.

Chris, Steve, John and myself were looking forward to a pleasant evening, we had met outside the ice rink where we trying to decide what we should do.

A newly registered VW van pulled onto the slip road outside the ice rink and stopped.

Our friend Tony was in the front passenger seat along with the two young men that the van belonged to, well to be more accurate; to a father of one of them.

Tony was well known for his fearless bravado and if anyone wanted a fight Tony was the man to confront.

For some vague reason it was decided that Chris, Steve, John and myself would get into the back of the van and join the three others for a drive, just for something to do.

So we got in.

The back door was closed behind us and the driver started the ignition.

The bad boys extracted themselves from the queue in a well-planned manoeuvre and charged at the van.

The people in the queue stared in disbelief as the onslaught began.

Through the front windows of the vehicle the bad boys started thrusting in daggers.

They formed a vicious human cordon around the van and from inside it we could not understand why or what was happening to us, the banging and kicking from outside accentuated frighteningly inside and I could see sharp - blades jabbing through the half open windows as Tony started kicking the hands that held the weapons. I shouted,

"Get us out of here, drive off"

Chris screamed,

"I want my mummy"

There was a shattering of glass as the back window exploded and a brick landed inside the van.

It was an incredibly frightening moment that none of us would ever want to re-live and why it happened is still a mystery.

We managed to escape by reversing the van at high speed and driving to the nearest police station.

Not one piece of glass was left intact on that van and the poor driver had to go home and explain to his father how the van had been wrecked. Luckily no one was injured but the police told us to 'go away.' So we did just that, we returned to the ice rink on that same night, because we were intent on visiting, the swish ultra - fashionable night club that was attached to the ice rink; The Bali Hai.

*   *   *

My little brother Phil was twelve years of age when he started receiving ice skating lessons on the young blades courses at the ice rink and I was thrilled that his instructor was Diane.

Diane went on to marry my good friend Marshall and it has to be said that I have never witnessed as dedicated a group of sportsmen and women as Diane and her instructor colleagues.

I would arrive at the ice rink at seven thirty am and at other times I would finish work at midnight or later but no matter when, those dedicated skaters would be there training, practising and perfecting their ice dancing skills. On the other hand, when the figure skaters weren't training it would be the hockey club or the speed skaters and sometimes the barrel jumpers.

 Sitting up in the grillette late at night and looking down on an empty ice rink with nothing in sight but the dedicated ice dancers gliding gracefully around the rink was a privilege.

 Watching a breath taking Biellmann spin or side by side shotgun spin was really impressive, until the instructor would stop his or her pupils, tell them it was not quite right and to 'please try again' sheer dedication.

 When I watched the speed skaters practise late at night it was impressive stuff.

 They swung one arm backwards and forwards with the other arm folded behind their back as they leant forward, almost touching the ice with their fingers eventually swinging into a rhythm that saw their muscular legs thrusting back and then forward as they pushed forwards with their toes until their constant momentum swung like a pendulum and I could see from their expressions as they whizzed around the outer edge of the rink, that these were probably the best moments of their lives they must have felt that they had become one with the ice as they swept all before them cruising through their gears, speeding round and round, real contentment.

The Streatham Redskins, the resident Ice Hockey team had recently regained a residential venue slot and Sunday nights were hockey Nights.

John and Pauline and Alec and Kathy were the driving force that had managed to revive the Hockey team and with the help of Nick one of MECCA's up and coming director's a new initiative had begun.

A large brewery sponsored the Ice Hockey League and the Redskins even managed to sign two wonderfully talented players from abroad Gary and Robin who added to an already talented side that featured Alec and Nicky and Brian to name but a few.

I felt privileged that on some hockey match nights I was able to do the MC announcing. Many of the refereeing decisions were booed or applauded by the hundreds of ice hockey fans that travelled from all over the country to watch this magnificent exciting sport and sometimes it got really tough.

The thing about this, about the actual hockey players, is that a lot of them were 'home grown' and had started out their skating lives as young inexperienced skaters, some of them had even worked in the skate hire.

*   *   *

1973

Sitting in a dining room with thirty five others, above my mum and dad's greengrocers on that particular evening was not really where I wanted to be.

My sister had fallen foul of the cursed Broxenia.

Even during the 1970's certain things were frowned upon by the Greek community.

There was no way a respectable young Greek Cypriot girl should be seen to enjoy the freedom of a full social life, or indeed to make innocent friendships with the opposite sex un-chaperoned.

It was not allowed to happen.

It was a shame but that is how it was and although my sister had never socialised with anyone but her school friend Mandy; It had been decided that the time had come.

A marriage had been arranged for her and her betrothed by family acquaintances, she was still only eighteen years of age.

That was how it was then and there was nothing that she or I could really do to halt proceedings.

After a small engagement party the date was set.

This was the evening reception. They had married earlier in the day.

I tried to hide my disappointment and I had also asked her to think about not going through with it but Androulla quite rightly said to me,

"I really don't have many other options do I?"

She was right there were no other practical options, not in those days anyway.

You just could not argue with family over such traditional family customs, it was pointless.

Now I must tell you about Harry.

At the time he was sixteen years of age and he had come along with his mother and sister to the celebratory wedding evening, indeed it was his mother Christina that had arranged the Broxenia.

I had met Harry a few times and we had acknowledged each other but we were not really on speaking terms. I reckon there were about sixty people there that night, but Harry really caught every ones attention.

He was a pleasant and polite young man, very broad shouldered and about five feet and nine inches tall. He had a thick - set build without being overweight and I imagined that it would be very hard to knock him over in a game of British bull dog he was (and still is)solid.

After an hour of eating and talking and some light conversation, everything seemed to be going pretty well and I decided to play some of my pop records, just to add a bit of extra spice to my sister's wedding night.

After a few records, I decided on *Stir it up* by *Johnny Nash*, why not?

All the guests were seated and talking to one another happily and I saw Harry stand to his feet and walk slowly across the room.

I watched as he walked up to a young girl, whose name I have conveniently forgotten as he leant forward like an army officer and offered her his arm and said,

"Would you like to dance?" They had never met before.

I giggled, what the hell was he doing,' this aint no disco,' I thought.

We were sitting in a living room being polite to one - another in honour of my sister Androulla and her new husband Andrew's wedding just listening to my music was all that I had intended, not moving to it.

Was Harry going to attempt some kind of barn dance, or even worse, a Greek style reggae dance?

The girl, who I think was about fifteen at the time; surprised us all by standing up and accepting. All heads turned towards them and the small talk ceased abruptly as everyone stared.

I am positive that her parents were in shock as Harry grabbed her by the waist and pulled her tightly towards him, there was no cutting corners as far as Harry was concerned and to give her full credit, the young girl reciprocated with an equally tight grip.

It would not have been possible to put a thin piece of paper between them.

The face of the Greek girl's father acquired a fiery red complexion as everyone watched Harry's impromptu serenade. They clung to each other as if their lives depended on it.

That was it for me, enough was enough.

When it got to seven thirty I told my sister that if she did not object I would be going to the ice rink. She smiled and I am sure she was thinking,

'Wish I could come along with you.'

The ice rink was for me as I am sure, for many others like me, my place of salvation.

You could leave your troubles at home and once you were on the ice, skating around the rink to a popular tune just placed you in a wonderfully different place.

On that particular night, three or four 'mad' skaters, as I called them, were feeling full of energy as they sprayed me and several other skaters with large amounts of melted ice as they skidded and raked their blades into the ice, coming to an abrupt stop in order to intentionally soak us.

 One of them shoved me in the back and I fell forward on my face. My front tooth cracked and broke in half.

 'Something to remember my sister's wedding day by' I thought, there was really nothing I could do about my tooth or my sister's marriage.

*   *   *

1977

Maurice Wise was a red coat and he was very good at his job.

 When I was younger he had banned me from skating on several occasions for going too fast.

 Red coats were ice supervisors that skated around the ice rink policing fast and dangerous skaters in order to avoid accidents.

 They were necessary.

Looking down from the balcony I could see that things were getting out of hand and poor Maurice was being taunted by nine tearaway skaters.

He was trying to catch up with them, but they were quick, skilful and crafty.

As floor supervisors the brothers Peter and Jack assisted Maurice.

They walked onto the edge of the ice pad and pulled the tearaways off, banning them for the evening.

The nine boys all protested their innocence, but we held fast and insisted that they keep off the ice.

The problem festered and during the next few weeks it became increasingly dangerous for members of the public to skate because of the tearaways; whose numbers were growing by the day.

It was the weekend after Halloween.

The ice rink was full to capacity and Maurice was the only ice supervisor on duty.

Jack, Peter and the other floor supervisors were too busy with queue control to assist the ice staff.

As I looked down at proceedings and at the kamikaze skaters disrupting and knocking other skaters over, I made a snap decision and made an announcement over the tannoy system which cut through the pop music so that all that could be heard was yours truly,

"Attention please, we are currently recruiting for Ice supervisors and if any of you are interested in wearing a red coat in order to help maintain ice skater safety, please come up to the office area in the next ten minutes"

I walked out of the office where the microphone was situated and during the three paces it took me to reach the door that led out onto the balcony of the ice rink. I heard a tumultuous clanging noise.

I opened the door, the noise was the result of several people; all wearing ice skates racing up the metal nosed steps that began on the ground floor and led up to the balcony area near the office.

There were two females and nine males; walking the best they could on their ice skates as they rushed towards me.

"Stop" I shouted, frightened that I was about to be trampled on.

The volunteers stopped and gathered around me. I gave them all a little pep talk and told them what I expected of them, I knew them all.

The nine male volunteers were the very people that I was concerned about, the reckless skaters who had forced me take action and recruit help.

Amongst them were Toots - Michael - Chris McDonnell and Steve Abbs

I told them about their new responsibilities.

Each one of them nodded obediently and then informed me that they really weren't villains of the ice . . . they were just converts to travelling at high speed on the ice.

It's true . . . nothing in sport compares to moving under your own steam at speeds that are at times faster than a motor bike or car . . . the exhilaration and that perpetual achievement never leaves you and I can only begin to imagine how amazing it would be to do all that with a goal to aim at whilst sweetly striking the rubber puck with a hockey stick or racing at speed in a speed skating race.

My goodness what an effect the donning of a red jacket had.

On the back of each jacket that I handed the volunteers were the gold coloured words:' Ice Supervisor'.

I swear that as I watched them walk back down the stairs - they were radiating the nearest thing that could be called - visible pride.

I guess they must all look back on that particular period of their lives and appreciative just how good they were at carrying out their skilled and dangerous ice supervision.

All of us that skated at Streatham recall so many interesting characters and incidents and it would take me another one hundred and sixty pages to list all the names. But I have to tell you about my most efficient ice skating stewards . . .

Looking down from the balcony on a busy disco evening always gave the precise information that I needed to evaluate on how well the 'traffic' was moving.

A swathe of skaters moved in an anti – clockwise direction.

There were at least fifteen hundred people on the ice and you could spot the novices who held on to the nearby barrier for all they were worth. Eventually over days or weeks they would teach themselves the skills of balance and control and move on up the scale from novice to 'skater'

Perhaps that explains why everyone who skated - loved the sport so much.

Some of us . . . like me . . . had not experienced such an enthralling feeling in life as that single self satisfying achievement that began with repeatedly stumbling and falling onto a cold slab of frozen water . . . but we persevered . . . because everyone around us was moving with such ease and if they could do it then so could we . . . and we kept going, each one of us whether reading this story or the friends featured in it - eventually reached a standard of skating that was truly incredible and I say to all of you . . . normal fun loving skaters or our ice superstars . . .

'Well done you on such an incredible feat' Ice skating is not easy.

I leant on the balcony rail and watched for several minutes as the new ice supervisors skated around the Ice rink, carefully and proudly wearing their jackets.

Within seconds they began instructing other skaters to slow down or to skate in the proper direction, anti - clockwise.

Calm and order were restored. It was nice to see that my plan had succeeded and in my time as acting general manager at the rink these new volunteers became the best I had seen . . . I know there were others before them and since.

On one busy Wednesday evening I looked down and spotted a young man weaving in and out of the skaters at breakneck speed. He moved quickly and dangerously stopping abruptly and spraying ice over skaters as he was forced to brake by slower more cumbersome skaters. He was reckless as he moved like a pinball through the slow ice traffic and he would have gotten away with it if not for the efficient partnership of ice stewards Steve Abbs and Chris McDonnell two young men that policed the ice so well.

When Steve and Chris were on the ice I never worried about ice safety, they formed an excellent marshalling partnership that somehow kept all the ice pad under their control and they seemed to do it with ease, they were excellent ice stewards and . . . they captured the rogue pinball moving skater, I was incensed by his dangerous actions so I decided to have a chat with him.

The young man was apologetic and cheeky. He was a great example of the effect ice skating at speed had on individuals who had discovered the ability to 'fly' like a bird across a frozen expanse.

That young man's name was Steve James and after a long chat, he too was given a red jacket and not only did he become one of the ice steward greats he also went on to become one of the stars of the Streatham Redskins ice hockey team I had the pleasure of also meeting Steve's mother: Jan (a truly wonderful parent who always put her son first) she lovingly ensured that he was given every chance to evolve his talents as Jan sometimes worried about his uncapped energies . . . until that single and pivotal moment in time . . . the very first . . . perhaps accidental or fortuitous moment that he decided to step onto the ice.

That is how ice skating at Streatham affected us all, it was a unique lesson.

Nowadays I am truly honoured to read on social media (and I have bumped into him a couple of times) how well Steve James has progressed in his life, he used to tell me when he was a young lad how he wanted to be a fireman . . . well he did just that and . . . became a Chief fire station officer and although he took early retirement Steve is still very active in organising emergency voluntary aid on many occasions.

Well done Steve, we (the ice skating family) are extremely proud of you.

*   *   *

I have seen war films that start with scenes showing heavily armed soldiers kitted out with heavy duty armour, sitting patiently inside an armoured personnel carrier, facing each other with a look of kill or be killed prominent in their eyes.

The same can be said for some of the supporters of a Birmingham Ice Hockey club, who travelled down by coach to follow their Ice Hockey team which were playing the Streatham Redskins that Sunday evening.

The game was contested at an explosive pace. No quarter was given as player after player met his opponent full on.

Both teams fought for every inch of ice, the referees had a busy evening as fight after fight broke out against the barriers between rival players.

The Redskins goalie Brian had a famous night and ultimately helped the redskins to win that game, much to the disappointment of the Birmingham supporters.

After the game the visiting supporters took to the ice.

That night produced more trouble than any other session I can remember as fight after fight broke out between rival hockey supporters and it was fortunate for Streatham Ice Rink that those nine former tearaways and their colleagues who had recently become redcoats had managed to maintain some kind of control until the evening session finished. Steve Abbs and Chris McDonnell were true saviours - it was a great relief to watch the away supporters board their bus back home.

*   *   *

It seems to me that the Ice Rink had an agenda all of its own when it came down to relationships.

Most of us were fortunate enough to meet our future partners there and also to cement ever lasting friendships with hundreds of others, friendships that are still as strong to-day.

Not forgetting the fact that our younger friends and relatives followed in our footsteps, such as my little brother Phil and my sister Androulla's boys George and Spiros.

The children of the Speed skaters, the Ice Hockey Club members and the figure skaters families, they all went on to make us proud.

I remember Alan and Debbie, Dianne's pupils and a host of other dedicated skaters that achieved championship status through their sheer dedication and today also, their children are carrying the Streatham Ice Rink flag.

Disc Jockey Memphis loved by everyone at the rink (really should have gone on to greater fame with such a great DJ voice and a wonderful talent for entertaining) agreed to attend my wedding day to my lovely Rita in Liverpool.

We got married in the city's Catholic Cathedral, the reception was held in a nearby hotel and obviously the DJ was . . . Memphis.

We had to take the Ice Rink atmosphere with us everywhere we went.

*   *   *

Young Mickey Carter had pleaded with me on several occasions to give him a chance to become a DJ at the ice rink and after several refusals I relented.

Mickey Came out of the skate – hire, to take over a Saturday afternoon slot and I have to say Mickey Carter was a brilliant Disc Jockey.

I remember his first DJ session and the unforgettable smile across his face - after that there was no holding him back. Jandy and Memphis helped him along at times but after a while he became an expert DJ. Mickey Carter went on to DJ many sessions at the ice rink and also hosted several sessions in the Bali Hai night club.

Mickey helped to 'hold the DJ fort' together at the ice rink for many years and was more than a member of the exclusive Streatham Ice Rink family, he was everything that epitomised the effect that the unexplainable Ice rink atmosphere had on us all, we still miss him very much today.

*   *   *

When it comes to perfection *Dancing on Ice* can never compare to *The Streatham Open Festival* at Streatham Ice Rink.

Weeks of preparation and planning went in to organising and hosting this annual competition that included the grading and testing of figure skaters and dancers, all by World Class judges.

A million miles away from the hustle and the bustle of a noisy pop filled evening session, this was a four day event that focused on pure ice skating skills.

The judging began at seven thirty am and continued until six thirty in the evening, as exhausting for the competitors as it was for the judges. The atmosphere was tense and very quiet as audiences watched the routines being performed throughout the day.

The only amplified sounds that one could hear were the occasional dance soundtracks and the applause when the judge's marks were awarded.

On the final evening of each festival, usually a Thursday evening, the ice dancers competed keenly and for some of the routines David Lowe played the Hammond organ majestically as they performed.

Strangely enough the same Saturday of that week heralded the famous and frantic, All Nighter.

An all - night session was usually held once a year and involved the participation of the national youth club federation of England.

From ten thirty in the evening, coaches full of young adults began to arrive and park up on Streatham high Road. On this one particular all night skate there were sixty coaches full of would be skaters.

The public were not allowed inside unless they arrived with one of those youth organisations.

Everything inside the rink had to be prepared for the busy evening ahead.

Staffing levels were extremely high, eighteen floor supervisors and twelve ice supervisors were on call. In the skate hire there were ten skate hire lads on duty and on the stage there were three disc jockeys.

At eleven o clock that evening we opened the doors and managed to get all the youth members inside the rink and onto the ice for their scheduled start time of midnight.

It was going really well.

Amongst the ice stewards were, Stephen 'Abbo' Abs his colleagues; Trevor and Les Mead, Toots, Ricky and his wife Tina. Maurice, Matt and many others, they were excellent and all skated with sharp awareness helping the learner skaters and quickly picking up others that had fallen before someone else's skating boot ran over and chopped off their fingers.

The ice supervisors were brilliant.

It was going so well until, quite innocently and in the name of friendly rivalry one of the DJ's; Roland began asking the skaters for the loudest supporter's cheers as he went through a list of football teams.

The ice supervisors were the first to become embroiled in the fights as they tried to separate the opposing supporters, stewards were running everywhere to try and contain the outbreak of fights.

I watched from the balcony as a formation of fights began to spread across the ice rink like a Mexican fight wave. I hurried to assist the supervisors, miraculously no one was seriously injured but the fighting and arguing continued for several hours.

Finally at six thirty am, the all night skate was over and the skaters had departed.

As far as I know during my time there, football teams were never again mentioned by DJ'S.

*   *   *

In 1979 the ice rink had to close for the renewal of plant machinery.

For eighteen months John, Gary and myself along with Sally the night watch lady and Don the schools supervisor went into the ice rink every day.

It was sad to see the ice rink unused and deserted.

The shouts of joy from skaters mixed in with the sounds of dance music and pop evening sessions were becoming a distant memory.

A slow trickle of curious and sometimes desperate people would occasionally call at the front door of the ice rink foyer; from instructors to ice hockey skaters and ice speed skaters.

Some would start conversing with polite conversation before quickly getting to the point:

'When is it opening again?'

A lot of them were extremely concerned that the eventual outcome would be catastrophic: That the ice rink would remain closed until it was demolished - eventually becoming a block of flats or even worse, a huge supermarket!

'Nonsense' I would say, everything will be fine, I felt like the Ice rink agony aunt but at the back of my mind I too was concerned that perhaps things might not go the way that we hoped.

They were troubled times not just for the supporters of the ice rink but also for the rest of the country.

Civil unrest was rife as a result of inequality and hardships suffered by ethnic minorities and under - privileged groups around the country.

The outcome of the protests resulted in sometimes bloody and spontaneous riots across major cities around the country.

Inevitably the effect of the breakdown in law and order meant that police forces around the country were seen by demonstrators as the public enemy.

Thinking about it now, it was probably a fortunate coincidence that the Ice rink was closed at that time. Based on previous flashpoints at the rink I feel sure that some twisted logic by determined militant types could have resulted in a riot or worse at the ice rink.

To my surprise exactly the opposite actually occurred.

It was another mundane day; going to work at the inactive ice rink.

I looked out across the dry expanse that was once a gleaming lake of polished ice that had now become a vast flat lump of dry dusty concrete, still chalky white from its original painted colour.

Don informed me that there was a telephone call on hold for me,

One of the *MECCA* director's had arranged for the building to be used as an emergency feeding base for the police troops and that police staff were on their way to survey and plan catering operations at the rink. For us, the handful of remaining staff, this was something positive and even exciting.

I imagined that perhaps the police officers would be given the use of the Grillette restaurant and its kitchen - along with the two licensed bar areas.

If that was the plan, I guessed that there would be a shift rotation of perhaps one hundred visiting officer's at a time or something like that.

The first member of police staff to visit was Ian; a police employee who was in fact one of their gas and plumbing contractors, he was a friendly person aged about forty and keen to get his work done.

Ian took a look around the outside of the ice rink and then advised me that he would be setting up a kitchen in a large *portakabin* outside the ice rink; near the middle right hand fire exit doors.

Who was I to object?

Two days later at twelve thirty, a police superintendent entered the ice rink, we had a brief conversation and he told me that he would be bringing his men in.

So John and Gary opened the glass entrance doors to the rink and then, we stood back and out of the way, as fifteen hundred uniformed police men and women walked through the doors of the ice rink and made their way out on to the white chalky pad that used to be covered with ice.

Row upon row of trestle tables, each with eight chairs, had been laid out across the pad.

We looked down from the balcony as the efficient police catering services swung into action.

For the first time in months we could hear social activity coming from the arena, it was not the sounds of joyous skaters but those of fifteen hundred police officers, talking and laughing as they had their lunch.

When they had finished their meals they vacated their seats and left the rink, I noticed that many of them had picked up white chalk marks on their dark blue uniforms.

Almost within seconds they were replaced by a further fifteen hundred officers - and so it went for a few days until one tragic Friday morning.

It was eight fifteen in the morning.

I met Ian the police plumber at the front entrance and we agreed that he would walk around the outside of the building to the *portakabin* while I grabbed the huge bunch of security keys and went to open the fire exit door from within.

That is exactly what we did.

The silence from within the inactive ice rink was ruptured by the jangling of my keys.

I could hear Ian outside, unlocking the *portakabin* as I fiddled with the many keys to find the right key for the padlock and eventually I unlocked it.

I pushed against the metal black bar on the emergency exit door and opened it.

The door swung open for a few inches as I pushed the metal bar.

Unexpectedly, a thunderous booming noise erupted like a blast from a naval gun.

The door felt heavy and recoiled inwards knocking me to the ground. I sat on the floor of the ice rink walk way, dazed but unhurt.

"Help . . . help me . . . please . . . help"

The cries came from outside, I stood up opened the exit doors and ran outside.

The first thing I noticed was that the entire side wall of the *portakabin* hut nearest to the ice rink had collapsed it had been blasted away from the rest of the hut and was leaning precariously towards me.

Ian walked into view; the poor man was walking nervous and screaming,

"Help me help me."

He was on fire from the top of his head and all the way down to his toes.

I was lost for words.

"Get it off me, get it off me . . . PULL IT OFF . . . PULL IT OFF . . . " He was not asking me , he was ordering me, . . . shouting angrily for me to pull the smoking nylon string vest away from his back . . . so I did . . . I appreciate now that in such an emergency you are not meant to do that.

The rest of his clothes, apart from his underpants had already peeled away and lay smouldering in small piles on the ground.

I took my jacket off and placed it around his shoulders I laid Ian on the ground and ran for all my life was worth . . . to the office area . . . to the phone and . . . dialled . . . nine . . . nine . . . nine.

I must have told them to get an ambulance to Streatham ice rink in the most urgent fashion, because - by the time I had run back down the stairs and outside to the *portakabin* the ambulance had arrived.

I will never understand how that ambulance managed to get there so quickly.

After the accident, no more police troops were fed at the ice rink and once again we went back into hibernation, I could not see how Ian would have been able to recover from such a horrendous accident.

*   *   *

Finally, a phone call informed me that the building contractors would be arriving at the ice rink one Monday morning to begin repair and refurbishment work on the disabled ice pad.

Fantastic news that John, Gary and all of us were pleased to hear.

A lot of the ice skating instructors who had been out of work due to the closure of the ice rink were told of the progress thanks to their colleague Peter Webb.

Peter had visited the ice rink on most days during the closure and we had kept him informed of any positive news.

So the word got around and once again it felt like a slight buzz of exhilaration was flowing through the dormant under soil cooling pipes of the ice rink.

On that Monday we waited anxiously for the contractors.

John and Gary debated what would arrive first; heavy machinery, a team of surveyors or perhaps just a *jcb* digging machine.

We waited and while John and Gary were busy carrying out last minute checks on the ice rink's plant and machinery to ensure easy access for the contractors, I could not keep away from the entrance foyer, waiting for their arrival.

At eleven thirty while I was pacing up and down the inside of the foyer looking out towards Streatham high road in the hope that a fleet of builders would arrive. A tall thin unshaven man with long straggly black greasy unkempt hair walked slowly past the ice rink doors.

As he walked, he turned his head towards me and nodded. I did not know him but I did notice that he was carrying a bulky Sainsbury's carrier bag in each of his hands. I nodded politely hoping he would move out of my line of vision so that I could carry on with my search for the imminent arrival of the builders.

The tall man stopped.

He turned, faced me and smiled at me through the glass door revealing cracked front teeth and glaring blood shot eyes.

Again I nodded politely.

He placed one of his carrier bags on the ground and with his free hand pushed at the door in an effort to open it.

Instinctively I took one step back.

"It's locked" I said

"Will you let me in please?" He asked quietly.

I was confused. But being a curious type of person I needed to find out what he wanted. So I unlocked the door and he walked in to the foyer, smiled at me and in a broad southern Irish accent he said,

"I am here to begin work to-day."

"Doing what?" I asked him.

"I don't quite know." He said.

"I'm sorry, but we are closed, there are no jobs available at present" I told him.

"Oh" he said. The poor man sounded confused.

"Who told you there was any work here?" I said, beginning to feel sorry for him.

"The job agency" He said.

"I think someone is trying to wind you up." I told him.

"No . . ." He said

" . . . They told me to get here and begin work on digging up a bit of the concrete so that Laing's the contractors could begin an inspection."

Well, I was speechless.

 John and Gary came to my aid.

They took him inside the ice rink and led John the labourer out onto the dry concrete pad.

 I watched as John the Irish labourer stood at the centre of the large concrete pad, he did not look amused as he scratched his head, trying to figure out what to do.

John the engineer took the initiative and led him over to the pit area where, during active ice time the *Zamboni* machine would dump all its ice and water after cutting and re - skimming the surface.

 "If you are going to dig anywhere, you had best start here near the pit, it might help the inspection." John and Gary told him.

So without further ado Irish John took his pickaxe out of a carrier bag and started breaking up a three foot square section of concrete.

*   *   *

As the re - building program commenced we witnessed the emergence of the new ice rink, it was a great experience for us and we were fortunate enough to have an input into the design of the new ice rink along with the help of MECCA'S director Nick.

When I re-opened the doors of Streatham Ice Rink the first night queues snaked around the building towards Streatham Bus Garage, ninety percent of those people were the same loyal followers that had frequented the ice rink before its closure.

It was great to see them again.

*   *   *

Christmas Eve came around pretty quickly.

It was always a busy night at the Ice rink due to the fact that all the regulars wanted to be there with their friends, the rink meant that much to them; especially at Christmas it was their second and to many of them, their first home.

I was notified by Patricia the cashier that I had a telephone call, which I duly took.

It was probably the best phone call I have ever taken; a man's voice said;

"Is that Theo?"

"Yes" I replied hurriedly, wanting to get back to the skate hire.

"Merry Christmas mate." He said.

"Who is this?" I asked impatiently.

"Theo, you might not remember me, but this is Ian, the met police man, the plumber, remember me? I . . . I . . . just want to thank you for saving my life"

I was elated.

The poor man had survived his ordeal, he was still being treated in a special burns unit at Roehampton Hospital but after several months, he had pulled through and was to eventually lead as normal a life as possible.

He told me that the accident had been caused by someone leaving a gas cylinder on throughout the night which had unfortunately ignited when he had turned the light switch on that fateful morning.

If not for all those dozens of keys on the key ring I would have opened that fire door much quicker and I would have been out there with him as the explosion occurred. I am pretty sure that neither us of would have survived.

*   *   *

1972

It was a desperate situation. If they caught any of us, there was a high probability that we would end up with a broken limb or worse.

Our lives were in danger but we were not going to give up until the very end.

It was the most dangerous thing that we did but we wanted it and although tensions were extremely high the spectators were either cheering or booing us.

Memphis orchestrated events from the stage.

In the middle of the rink stood Derek Gascoigne, John Turvey and Bob Young, three of the fastest and most versatile skaters you could ever encounter. The 'game' was British Bulldog and no mercy was shown by anyone.

A hundred of us, all male, were lined up on the foyer end of the ice rink and John and Rob stood in the centre all we had to do was skate to the opposite end of the rink without getting tagged by them if we did, then we had to join their army of taggers.

Memphis counted down,

"Three . . . two . . . one"

He blew a whistle and we were skating cautiously towards the other end trying to avoid Derek, John and Bob.

It was always wise to let them chase other skaters in order to find an escape route through the melee.

The first charge was easy, after that it was mayhem.

People were grabbed by their arms, their waists, their legs or even their heads as they were snagged.

For some it was full on as they were brought down while skating at high speed which meant that they somersaulted or bounced into the air before landing heavily onto the hard ice.

It was extremely dangerous and I am sure that British Bulldog in that original form is probably banned nowadays but it was great fun and when Derek and John and their like; who were experienced barrel jumpers were on the charging end, they would not be caught until last.

They would zig - zag sideways, inching towards the centre, waiting and biding their time.

On one particular night John was the last man standing.

On the centre there were at least one hundred skaters waiting to tag him and finish the bulldog.

There was nowhere for John to escape to.

He started to weave across the rink from side to side as slowly he began inching his way towards the middle of the ice and the defensive line of taggers who were waiting to bring him down.

We held our line, there were no gaps and John would surely have to collide with one of us.

He flicked his heels outwards as he lowered his shoulders and swung his arms quicker and quicker, building up the momentum as he hurtled towards us, our formation broke as we tried to advance on him, John skated around two and then three taggers; all that stood between him and the safety of the opposite barrier was yours truly. I spread my arms and held my position as a few more taggers filled in the gaps either side of me.

John charged and as I reached out to grab him, he barrel jumped over our heads.

It was breath taking and the barrel jump he had executed took him at least three inches over our heads. He landed; incredibly, on both skates and glided across to the safety of the barrier.

When the boy's British bulldog was over, the girls did it all over again in similar breath taking fashion with members of the girl's speed team nearly always amongst the winners.

*   *   *

During the 1960's and the early 1970's the busy main high road from Streatham Hill through to Streatham Common was known as MECCA's Golden Mile; due to the entertainment and leisure business that were operated there by MECCA LTD.

There was the bingo hall (which had been a theatre) and the famous Locarno Dance Hall with its exclusive night club, the Stork Club.

Also there was the Streatham bowling alley and further along the road there was the Golden Nugget Casino and about a mile down the road from there was: The Silver Blades Ice Rink and The Bali Hai.

Add two major cinema houses The ABC and The Odeon plus several restaurants and pubs and Streatham Library along with the wonderful *John Lewis Pratt's* department store to complete the picture and hopefully you will understand why the residents of Streatham were quite happy with the amenities they had at their disposal in Streatham.

When I was three years of age my father George was the head waiter at the Stork Club, which was part of The Locarno and my mother was busy working from home making dresses on a very noisy *Singer* sewing machine that in turn was embedded into a huge heavy wooden table. It was louder than a street workers pneumatic drill and I longed to be older so that I could go to school with my sister Androulla so as to escape that terrible droning noise.

*   *   *

Effie, my mother took her foot of the sewing machine foot pedal, stood up and decided it was time we went shopping.

At the bottom of Barcombe Avenue and on the opposite side of the main dual carriageway was John Sainsbury's; right on the corner of Streatham Hill and opposite the main line railway station.

It was a great store, Inside I would always stare in amazement at the countless trays of meat and bacon, so many different types of cooked pies and so much bacon; thin, fat, smoked, unsmoked, thick cut, thin cut, there were so many. I could read the numbers but not the words on the price tags that were poked into the meat displays; all hand written and I thought, very artistically done.

On that particular day I just stood and stared at the **Sainsbury's** staff in their straw boater hats as they served customers and weighed meat portions on those bubbly shaped weighing scales.

My little nostrils turned upwards as a handful of smoky bacon was placed on a square piece of greaseproof paper, the man behind the counter looked at the female customer as she scrutinised the weight of the bacon,

"Take a bit off, leave it or add a bit more." He asked her politely in a cockney voice.

The woman hesitated. I knew what he was asking her and I thought that she should definitely have a bit more, after all it looked scrumptious.

"How much does that come to?" She asked him.

"Just under a shilling" He said as he smiled and waited, the woman hesitated and the man sighed just a little as he tried to get a decision out of the customer, I for one could not wait any longer so I spoke out,

"More." I said.

They both looked down at me. The woman smiled and the man laughed. He looked at me and then behind me,

"Here, me little old mate . . ." He asked me.

". . . Where is your mother?"

I looked around and then looked further afield towards the outer reaches of the store, where was she? I could not see my mother anywhere.

That was it.

Panic set in as I ran around the store crying and looking for her, I even ran into the second part of the store that adjoined the cooked food hall.

I could not find my mother anywhere, she had simply forgotten about me as she started her walk back to our house.

For a three year old I think I was very thorough as I carried out an extensive search of the store by walking across the entire floor of Sainsbury's at least twenty times and before I knew it I was outside on the main street of Streatham Hill sobbing and shouting for my mother, I was absolutely certain that she was nowhere to be found.

What to do?

I looked at the main dual carriage way and the continuous fast traffic on the A23; one of Britain's busiest A roads was preventing me from running over to Barcombe Avenue, I knew the way home but I had never crossed a major road on my own, ever. None of the adults who were walking past me made any attempt to stop and find out why I was alone and so distressed.

So there comes a time in every person's life when that first important decision has to be taken.

For me, that decision came at the age of three; to cross the busy A23 road on my own.

Once I had made my mind up it was easy. I knew from the stories my family often told, that all vehicles were bad if they collided with people, especially yourself. There had been a spate of road traffic accidents on that stretch of road and my aunts and uncles were always commenting about 'the poor unfortunate person who had no chance after the bus had trapped them beneath its wheels'

So I knew that all vehicles were dangerous as I watched and waited.

Buses and trucks and several cars sped along the dual carriageway towards Brixton Hill and after a few minutes I continued to stare and concentrate as hard as I could, I saw that there was nothing coming in my direction, not even a bicycle.

My little legs ran as fast as they could and I made it safely across to the central reservation island where I stopped and then stared to my left, only one car passed as it headed towards the high road and then, it was completely clear.

I ran across the road and up Barcombe Avenue. I had made it and it felt fantastic, nothing could stop me as I ran all the way to the 57th house on the right; 114.

I knocked on the door and my auntie H opened the door quickly, she seemed upset and when she saw me she began to shout at me in a fast Greek dialect.

I replied in the best way that a three year old could.

Trust me reader, you do not want to know what an abandoned three year old is capable of saying, in Greek, after such a traumatic situation.

*   *   *

1971

My secondary school Dunraven was an OK type of school. Without telling you about the humdrum boring bits I will get straight to the point.

At the age of fifteen I had many good school friends, boys and girls and one of my best friends was Simon Mandry and boy, was he was a cool dude.

Simon was a young man who was fully in touch with the latest fashion and pop.

Somehow, Simon managed to keep himself and the rest of our school friends updated with the then trendy meaning of cool, all his opinions were hip and if you wanted keep up with modern teenage culture, then Simon was the boy to listen to on what was in, or what was out, if you know what I mean.

On one particular summers day in 1971 Simon Mandry arrived for the start of a normal school day and as he came into view, every single pupil in the playground area turned their attention towards him and stared.

"Hello mate." Simon said as he beamed a wide smile at me.

"Wow! What have you done to your hair Simon" I asked as I stared up at his new hair style.

"It's a *Rod Stewart* haircut Theodore, do you like it?" He asked me,

"Brilliant" I answered truthfully.

His normally light coloured thin and flat but quite long hair had been transformed into a classic *Rod Stewart* hair style. None of us had seen such a prominent, spikey and perfectly feathered hair style before.

Simon explained to me that this was THE haircut to have and had I not heard of Rod Stewart and Maggie? Well I had heard *Maggie May* played on the radio but to be honest I hadn't taken it as seriously as Simon.

After that day I purchased every Rod Stewart and the Faces record that was released. My only regret was that my tight curly hair would never allow for such a brilliant haircut.

1972

A few of us stood by the side of the stage. It was the area where we congregated after leaving the ice for a rest and somehow, as people at Streatham Ice Rink did, we had formed a cluster of friends that became close and reliant on each other.

The highlight of any evening at Streatham Ice Rink was when you were with your mates and there was several, probably hundreds of such groups.

Two of my Friends, Gwyneth and Eamon were enthusiastically asking the rest of us if we would like to accompany them to Brixton in the near future, to watch Rod Stewart and The Faces perform at a live venue. I said yes straight away.

It was a brilliant gig and I knew the words to every song that they performed.

We were near the stage and had a great view of their scintillating performance.

When Rod and the boys came back on for an encore, Rod performed his usual party piece and started kicking full sized lightweight footballs out in to the audience.

I jumped up and luckily caught one of the footballs. Gwyneth smiled,

"Well done." She said, but a second later a tall young man with a Rod Stewart haircut that was even more startling than Rod's snatched the ball from my hands.

"Hey" I shouted, that's mine.

"Not any more, now it's mine" He said, as he and his friends laughed and walked away with my football.

"Never mind" Gwyneth said, at least it was yours for a little while."

*   *   *

1978

Mesmerising moments in life are permanently etched, like blockbuster film trailers in my memory..

The first time I entered Santa's Grotto as a small child, or the first Christmas morning my sister and I woke up on and found toys for presents instead of boring pullovers or new shoes.

 Or the very first day at school or perhaps the very first time you saw a member of the opposite sex that you were really attracted to.

 Or the first time you dared to skate backwards at high speed during a speed skating session, reminding yourself not to fall over and embarrass yourself.

*   *   *

As I neared the main upstairs entrance the sound of pulsating disco music was leaking through to the stair well.

 A bouncer moved aside and with my friends we walked into . . .
The Bali Hai.

The perfect sound system delivered the most wonderful disco tune and believe it or not, the song that I thought was made for the Bali Hai was actually playing the words which I thought I heard:

Bali . . . Bali . . . Bali . . . Hai . . .

It took me a few weeks to realise that the words were from the *Earth Wind and Fire* song, *September* and the actual words which sounded like Bali Hai were in fact . . . Ba de ya.

It was the very first time I had ventured into The Bali Hai, the electrified atmosphere overwhelmed me. It was ten o'clock in the evening and the Bali Hai was already full to capacity.

A well thought out décor and dark soft background lights were dramatically interrupted by pulsating disco lights as the sharp silver reflections bounced off two large rotating crystal glitter balls.

' So this . . . ' I thought ' . . . is paradise'.

Every female in the club was drop dead gorgeous the girls all looked like they had just jumped off a fashion designer catwalk and the guys were all very smartly dressed.

Even though it was crowded it was a calm and happy place, chic and handsome with a touch of class.

And it was all about the music, if they weren't on the small dance floors moving to the beat they were standing around talking to each other whilst still swaying to the rhythm.

One of the greatest disc jockeys of The Bali Hai era was on the stage; Simon, he was a cool dude and he had his finger on the disco pulse that just kept you swaying if not dancing to the music.

1981

It had been a busy night at the Ice Rink and for some reason which is vague to me now, I had to finish work at the rink and make my way up to The Bali Hai to provide cover due to lack of management.

During the course of the evening I noticed a certain person in the club, he was quite distinctive looking and although he did not recognise me I remembered him straight away, the man from the Rod Stewart gig who had stolen my football and he still had that same hair style.

He was seated at a small table with a rather attractive young lady and as I strode over to them they were in the midst of a seemingly deep conversation.

 "Excuse me" I interrupted.

 He stared at me,

 "What?" He asked.

"The football, have you still got it?" I asked.

"What?" He said the word; what, in a long drawn out way, as if to say, I do not know what you are talking about and you are interrupting us.

 "The Rod Stewart football . . . from the concert."

He stared at me.

He pondered and then I could see that he had remembered.

 He smiled.

"Gave it to my kid brother, he took it to school with him and someone took it from him."

We both kept silent for a few seconds, I smiled,

"Okay, good to see you, have a good night." I said as I began to walk away.

 "Yeah ehm mate . . ." He called out after me.

". . . sorry and all that."

"Yeah no problem." I said and although I had achieved absolutely nothing, I felt good, as the James Brown record of the same name: *I feel good*, began to play.

*   *   *

The Ice rink always looked 'ship shape' the new halogen lights that hung above the ice took a bit of time to warm up when they were switched on in the mornings but when they eventually warmed to their task, the bulbs generated a lasting brightness that highlighted the design of the recently refurbished ice rink.

The Ice rink had an abundance of glass windows: The Grillette - The cocktail bar - The downstairs bar - The Skate accessories shop.

All of those glass panes had to be cleaned and maintained so that they were always sparkling and able to reflect the overhead lighting.

During one particular morning a representative of a window cleaning company asked if he could have a meeting with me, so I duly obliged and allowed him to enter the office area.

As soon as I saw him I knew who he was.

I led him into the office and waited for him to start talking and even though I knew him, he had not recognised me.

"Look ehm . . . Sir"

He called me Sir.

" . . . Thanks for seeing me. My company of which I am the owner would like to take over the contract for cleaning the windows of the ice rink, all of them."

I was polite and nodded positively as he pitched his company to me.

"We already have contracts with some of your sister branches . . ." he went on and on and persevered until he must have sensed that I had not been persuaded by his sales talk.

I watched him as he began to perspire and without warning he placed his hand inside his jacket and pulled out a plain unmarked brown envelope.

He smiled nervously as he walked over to my desk and placed the envelope down.

"Look, there is a hundred pounds in cash inside that envelope."

I stared at him as he continued,

"Every month, I will give you an identical envelope and there is no need to tell anyone, now how good is that?" He smiled.

I walked over to the desk picked up the envelope and handed it back to him.

"No thanks very kind of you though but definitely no."

His jaw dropped and he began to protest.

"If you don't mind Nick, I have things to do, so I will show you out."

I opened the door and led him out onto the balcony and then down the stairs.

"Wait . . ." He said

" . . . I never told you my name, how is it you know me?"

"How can I ever forget you Nick, but it is a pity you don't recognise me, last time we met, you were running the wrong way around a greyhound stadium track after you decided to change the result of the dog race."

There was a notable look of shock etched across Nick the Greek's face, he was older but still sweaty and still ugly and unshaven.

"Wait . . ." He stared as he recognised me,

"Why you're . . . you're George's little boy, I remember you now."

I stared back at him.

"Well . . ." He said quickly, I had best be going, say hello to your dad for me.

And with that Nick the Greek left hurriedly through the front doors of the Ice Rink.

As I went back to my office I smiled to myself at least the old goat was trying to earn a relatively honest living.

*　　*　　*

Along with Kathy and Alec Goldstone and John and Pauline Rost I was on the ice rink stage helping out with the announcements.

They were wonderful people and it should be mentioned that Alec's sincere efforts had contributed so much to the advancement of the Streatham Redskins ice hockey club in such a relatively short period of time.

In fact, Alec had only show an interest in ice hockey when his son Tony began playing the game at Streatham and after that, there was no holding him back.

Manager Alec Goldstone's determination for the club to succeed soon helped to drive the Streatham Redskins on to great success and that period was for many of us a golden era. A time that could only be experienced by being there and soaking up that hyper charged tension that was emitted by every hockey game.

I announced the team names:

"Brian Cox, Dave Rapley, Roger Walland, Richard Bacon, Nicky Iandoli, Trevor Cogan, Jason Wright, Steve James, Peter Quinney, Gary Cloonan, Gary Stefan, Erskine Douglas, Tony Goldstone, Mark Howell, Gary Brine, Glynne Thomas, Robin Andrew, Chris Leggatt, John Rost and Phil Adams."

While I announced the teams the coach Red Imrie paced nervously up and down the team enclosure, shouting out orders to his players and punching the palm of his own hand as he tried to drive home the urgency of his game play instructions as Alex Johnston added a few more observations.

Alec Goldstone kept moving around fidgeting in his chair, his nervous tension was beginning to worry me as I announced the names of the Nottingham Panthers team.

It was a vital league game and both teams needed the points.

I looked back at Alec and smiled, he always wanted the best from his team.

"Relax - it will work out just fine." I said as calmly as possible.

"I hope so Theo." He replied still moving around on his chair.

The loud blaring noise of the Klaxon signalled the beginning of the Ice Hockey Match between the Streatham Redskins and the Nottingham Panthers.

The noise of the ice hockey sticks clattering into each other could clearly be heard above the cheering spectators as just one hundredth of a second later, the black vulcanized rubber missile known as the puck, pinged across the ice.

 Game on.

The pace was frenetic, a typical high class game that saw both sides defending and then keeping possession as they controlled the puck with ease.

 Gary Stefan moved his long hockey stick with one hand, guiding the puck easily and with masterful contempt as he skated behind the net as the Redskins began to stealthily build on yet another attack.

Robin Andrew took a long pass from Gary Stefan and immediately pushed the puck forward onto empty ice.

Tony Goldstone sped forward and without hesitation seized his opportunity, he swung his stick and struck the puck as sweetly as you like.

The Nottingham Panthers net minder never even saw it flash past him as it created a bulge in the back of his net.

Truly one of the best struck shots I have ever seen in Ice Hockey.

The arena erupted with loud cheering as I heard Alec Pauline and Kathy jump up from their seats. It took a while for the crowd to quieten down before I could announce the number and the name of the Streatham Redskin goal scorer, Tony Goldstone.

It was a breath taking match that flowed over every inch of ice and as it sometimes happens during such an intense match, a little bit of fighting broke out between the two sides.

At one stage I think all the players on the ice became entangled with their opposite number as punches were thrown. Steve James and an opposing team player became entangled as they fought to reach the puck with their sticks, Steve's stick snapped in half; that seemed to be the catalyst that created a brief period of all out war.

Robin Andrew was furious at a high raised stick that came close to injuring his already damaged teeth and he retaliated by discarding his safety helmet in order to get a better view of his opponent before delivering a left hook.

It was a good punch as the guy on the receiving end fell backwards over the barrier. A hockey riot broke out as the referees who were sandwiched between the players tried to separate the warring sides.

Robin was struck around the mouth.

It is the most vivid photo that remains etched in my ice rink memory.

Robin's anger was out of control as he spat out his mouth guard yet there was nothing he could do to prevent the jet of crimson streaks of blood from spurting out and falling all over his mouth it looked like he had reached the fifteenth round of a heavyweight boxing match but he was clearly raring to finish the fight and hopefully the referee would allow the battle to continue.

As the game resumed the tension was unbearable.

During one of the final attacks David Rapley hit the puck with tremendous power as the puck clipped another player's hockey stick on the way towards the net which deflected the shot and then sent it on a vertical path.

The puck struck one of the large window panes that protected the spectators who were watching from inside the licensed bar area at the far end of the rink, the glass cracked but thankfully did not shatter.

As the seconds ticked away the Redskins were winning by just one point, they managed to hang on for one of the greatest victories I have ever been privileged to witness, the celebrations by Robin and his team were memorable, the entire stadium erupted with cheers and whistles and applause as I looked towards Robin Andrews, he smiled broadly as the blood continued to pump out of his mouth.

We miss Alec and Kathy Goldstone and all our departed hockey friends, none will be forgotten.

       *   *   *

The young woman turned her gaze deliberately towards the soldier and smiled.

He was a romantic at the best of times and even though he was in full army kit and dangerously armed he just had to smile back at her.

She was about to enter a cafeteria and deliberately stopped at the doorway to smile at him again. He had to talk to her, but his fellow infantryman Jennings nudged him a warning that he should keep his mouth shut. He ignored Jennings,

"Are you going to buy us a coffee then?" He asked her. She carried on smiling and flirted with him as she replied with a Dublin accent,

"Can't do that I'm afraid, I work here."

"Leave it H. Come on let's go." Jennings persisted.

"I am in love." He replied as he smiled back at the attractive brunette.

A Crack . . .

The high velocity bullet struck Jennings with devastating effect.

His knee cap shattered and the bone fragmented.

Some of the flying bone shards cut into Harry's face. Instinctively Harry shook his head and with the back of his hand wiped the tiny bits of blood away from his cheek.

Jennings collapsed from his injury screaming from the agonizing pain as he lay on the cold Belfast pavement.

"Bloody Hell" Jennings cried.

Harry swung his rifle behind his back, grabbed the back of Jennings tunic collar with one hand and dragged Jennings backwards until they turned the corner of the block.

Harry knelt down and applied a pressure bandage to Jennings wound.

"Okay mate, just breathe, we are out of their sights now here . . . press on this bandage as tight as you can, okay?"

Jennings breathing sounded laboured as he drifted in and out of consciousness,

"Bloody Hell Harry, they've fucked my knee right up mate."

"I know," Harry sighed.

Harry took an adrenalin jab from his kit bag and stabbed it into Jennings leg.

After a few seconds Jennings started to breathe easier,

"Thanks H."

"No problem mate." Said Harry as he swung his rifle back into his arms and pointed it protectively in front of him, he stood up and walked to the edge of the block, he looked around the corner and pulled back quickly as another shot rang out.

The snipers gunfire had ensured that there were no civilians anywhere to be seen. The pretty girl had run into the café.

"Coming from that hill at the back of the farm" Jennings warned.

"Yep, nothing we can do but wait here J"

The two infantry men only had to wait a matter of minutes before back up and an army ambulance arrived. The medics took Jennings and Harry away from the danger zone as an attack helicopter tried to flush out the sniper.

The Café was called The Rendezvous and Harry walked in there the very next day dressed in his civvies.

She was there, standing behind the counter, but this time she was not smiling.

"What can I get you" She asked without looking at his face.

"Coffee please" Harry asked politely.

The girl nodded and began pouring the coffee.

She placed the cup of coffee on the counter.

"You don't seem to be as happy as yesterday miss." Harry said

"Why should I be?" She answered abruptly.

Harry sighed,

"Could it be that you were just trying to keep us in one place while one of your friends tried to kill us then?" Harry said calmly.

"You want this coffee or not." She snapped.

Harry kept quiet.

"Get out. Get out now if you know what's good for you." She said in a slow deliberate tone.

Harry took the coffee and walked over to a table and sat.

There was no one else in the café except for Harry and the waitress.

Harry heard her talking to someone on the telephone - he waited.

Harry stayed put and after an hour five men entered the café tall rugged looking men, they moved quickly.

Three of them sat at Harry's table the other two sat behind him. The one who sat next to Harry warned him,

"Now you listen, you are within a hairs breadth of losing your life. You need to get up and get away from here and never ever return, do you understand?"

Harry stared at the man without replying.

He felt the nozzle of a gun pressed against the middle of his back. One of the men behind him spoke quietly;

"Or we can always arrange for you to disappear."

Harry put both of his hands on the table.

The five men were startled by the action and stood to their feet instinctively.

Harry looked at all five men,

"Good day gents." He nodded courteously and walked out of the café.

"Freaking idiot" One of the men shouted after him.

Harry went directly back to his barracks, he put on his full army kit took his army rifle and five extra magazine rounds and within twenty five minutes he was back at the Rendezvous café.

As he approached he could clearly see that the men were still sat at the same table, they had not expected him to return.

Harry could see them running for cover as he kicked out heavily and pushed the door open. He began firing his rifle even before he was inside and he fired off an entire magazine into the café. When all the bullets were spent Harry locked in another magazine and made sure he shot and ruined as much of the cafés furniture – walls - plumbing and electrics as possible.

When he finished he walked across to the bullet riddled counter and placed a coin by the cash register. On his way out he said; "Thanks for the coffee"

*   *   *

One Wednesday evening, an unexpected visitor walked into the ice rink foyer, it was my old acquaintance Harry the boy who had attended my sister's wedding reception.

But now he was a fully grown man. He told me that he had recently left the British Army after a stint in Ireland. In a round - about manner he revealed that he and the army had decided to part amicably before 'things got out of hand.'

At the time his referral to life as a soldier told me very little of what had happened to Harry during his army life but I guessed that somewhere beneath his calm composure and from what he had told me, there lay a simmering volatile temperament and all that Harry really needed from me was a favour, he needed a job as a floor supervisor.

So, yes, you guessed it, after a few words from myself on how I expected a supervisor to be calm and always helpful (to which Harry heartily agreed) I let him have a job.

Thank god.

*   *   *

There is a ten year age gap between my little brother Phil and me.

 So when I was a member of the ice rink management he was fortunate enough to enjoy his young teens with his own group of Ice rink friends and although I still do not know the majority of them, I am privileged that we are all still connected as Ice rink friends.

Phil used to help out a lot in the rink and like all of us he has many Ice rink tales to tell.

*   *   *

It was a Saturday evening and one of the many nights that we (MECCA) had promoted as a special feature. This particular promotion was one of my ideas and originally called,

 "Miss Sexy Legs"

We had three large advertising 'A' boards in the foyer, plus the glass show cases on the outside walls that prominently displayed forthcoming attractions and I arranged for the local artist that painted our posters to create an attractive pair of female legs wearing a pair of ice skates.

Such a campaign would not be allowed nowadays because it would be classed as chauvinistic and politically incorrect. Quit right too.

The posters looked great, until one of the *MECCA* directors, Michael Woods walked in on one of his many fleeting and unannounced inspection visits and he told me to change the wording on the posters immediately as the word 'sexy' was totally offensive.

I put the boards away until I received some stick over matching poster artwork that covered up the words 'sexy' with the word, 'lovely'

So 'Miss Lovely Legs night' was under way.

But on that particular evening session we were low on supervisors both on and off the ice.

I took my usual walk along the balcony to see if I could spot any problems.

Looking down at the ice rink I noticed the lack of ice supervision.

The smooth anti - clockwise movement of skaters was being constantly disrupted by several tearaway skaters who were skating through gaps at high speed and in the wrong direction, there were no ice supervisors on duty as the two guys who were designated to work that session had both called in sick.

With uncanny bad timing, an accident occurred on the ice.

A man had been barged over and had fallen heavily onto the ice bumping his head on impact.

Fortunately the ever reliable St John's ambulance representative was on duty and after careful examination she arranged the stretcher bearer volunteers to carry the man into the first aid room while I stood on the ice waving my arms out in a cross formation like a silly person as a warning to other skaters.

Then I had to get up to the office to use the telephone in order to call an ambulance, on my way there my brother Phil ran up to me with another warning;

"Theo, there's trouble brewing at the front."

"Phil, please do me a favour get a red jacket on and get someone else on there with you, there's no ice supervision whatsoever." I pleaded.

"Leave it to me." He replied.

When I finally reached the front of the ice rink the cashier Pat informed me that the skate hire staff were asking for more help as they were also short staffed and the queues of people that were waiting to be served were getting longer and longer.

At the front reception were; Jack, Peter and Brian and also Harry. Jack who was the head supervisor suggested that.

 "You stay here with Harry Theo and the rest of us will go downstairs and sort out the skate hire queues."

Good idea.

Harry seemed quite relaxed as he leant on the advertising 'A' board that displayed my 'Miss Lovely Legs' poster.

As a matter of fact he was so relaxed that he was holding and reading a paper back novel as he leant forward.

On the outside of the front doors I could see a gang of about fifteen young boys peering in through the glass.

We'd had trouble with them before and although we had tried to calm them and use diplomacy they were only ever intent on causing trouble.

I put their problems down to youthful testosterone levels and a misguided camaraderie to each other, but one thing was for sure on that particular night we were in trouble.

We could hear Memphis announcing the line - up of the miss lovely legs contestants and as usual he was doing an excellent job. But I was stuck right there in the front reception and I was worried that things were going to fall apart.

I made a decision that we always tried to avoid, I locked all the front doors except for one and I then picked up the telephone receiver in the cashiers kiosk and called the police.

The little gang members were venturing into the foyer via the only unlocked door, I kept pushing them back out one by one but as I managed to push one out, another squeezed past me and entered.

It was getting hectic. I looked at Harry he looked up from his book, stared at me for a second and then went back to his reading.

"Must be a good book" I shouted as I wrestled with another intruder.

"Not bad." He muttered without taking his eyes away from the book.

I locked the door.

Now they were all closed and no one could get in but the trouble was, I was breaking safety rules and there were only forty minutes remaining until the session ended.

I could hear Memphis crowning the Miss Lovely Legs winner and people could be heard cheering and applauding.

Almost miraculously the gang outside had disappeared from sight.

I opened one of the doors and went outside, they had all gone.

With my attention focused on the empty pavement I opened all the doors, ready for the large throng of skaters who would be leaving at the end of the session.

I pushed the bunch of security keys back under the protective cahier glass and smiled at Pat but before I could say 'thanks' I noticed the panic in her expression.

Pat was looking over my shoulder and I turned to see what it was that had alarmed her.

The fifteen gang members had entered the foyer and they were all making a bid to enter the building.

"Hey!. . . " I shouted at them,

" . . . Get out now"

They glared at me as one of them produced a flick knife which duly opened in an instant.

"What are you doing, you silly boy?" I said calmly.

He could not have been more than fifteen years of age.

He laughed as he placed the point of the blade against my throat and pushed.

An almighty explosive sound shattered the tension.

Knife boy and I turned our attention towards the source of noise and we saw Harry standing in full combat mode.

He had kicked miss lovely legs up into the air and the 'A' board had landed face down on the smooth polished floor, the impact of the board against the vinyl tiles had created the large cracking noise.

It took them and me by surprise, they all took a step back including knife boy.

Harry performed some kind of ritual with his hands and arms, waving them around like a Maori warrior while shouting at the top of his voice . . .

"Hee . . .ah . . ." several times, as he pointed his karate chop shaped hands at the gang members.

They backed of some more and before the situation could develop further, dozens of police officers invaded the reception area . . . every one of the gang members were rounded up, but the threatening knife was never found.

"Thanks Harry." I said.

"You're welcome." He replied politely.

"So . . . where did you learn those moves and those noises?" I asked him,

With a very serious and matter of fact expression Harry looked at me and said sincerely,

"Army training"

"Off course" I agreed and I walked up onto the balcony and looked out across the ice,

The Miss lovely legs competition had been and gone and every one was skating in an orderly clock wise motion.

In the centre policing the skaters and standing back to back, wearing their red ice supervisor coats were Les Mead and Phil, they had sorted out the ice skater problems while Jack Peter and Brian had leant themselves to the skate hire.

Harry had sorted out the front of house problem and had probably saved me from serious injury or worse.

*   *   *

1969

When I was twelve years of age I started going to the cinema on my own.

When I was seven years old my sister would take me along to the Saturday Morning matinee at the ABC in Streatham although there were two major cinemas in Streatham; The ABC and . . . The Odeon.

We both loved the spell binding and excellent age of children's cinema.

The ABC was just along the way from Streatham Hill and my sister Androulla who was just eight years of age would take me along on Saturday mornings and we would sit amongst a thousand screaming kids to watch a selection of films some good and some brilliant.

We absolutely loved the atmosphere; the intervals - the screaming uncontrollable children and the ice cream bombs raining down from the seats above and - just now and then we watched a good film.

As I was telling you . . . by the time I was twelve . . . we had moved down the road into Farm Avenue; just behind the Odeon Cinema and off Streatham High road.

The greatest film ever released . . . at that time . . . *The Battle Of Britain* was on at the Odeon . . . so I went along to the Cinema on my own, purchased my single ticket and went inside to sit and savour *The Battle Of Britain*.

The left hand side of the large theatre was empty . . . yippee.

I sat in the middle of the left hand section alone and secluded from the other cinemagoers who were seated in the right hand bank of seats.

I loved my own privacy.

 The film was shaping up brilliantly and I have to admit that I could not take my eyes off the screen, especially when the character played by the great *Susannah York* was in view.

Ms *York* had the most attractive personality on screen and the most magnificent eyes . . . I think I was hooked then and there on the actress Susannah York.

The Battle Of Britain was only about forty minutes done when it was interrupted . . . or should I say; I was interrupted.

He walked down the left hand aisle.

He was overweight - six feet tall plus a few more inches and he stopped at the end of my row of seats looked across at me and shuffled along the row until he claimed the seat on my left.

He flipped the seat down and stuck his fat behind on the seat.

Why me?

He wore a long green anorak and dark tinted spectacles and he had a large peanut shaped head.

You could not make it up!

This all happened at the precise moment that the great British actress *Susannah York* was giving her best performance in a crucial address to senior flight officers.

But . . . being quite aware that this was not a normal situation I had to turn away from Susannah.

I stood up and without a second glance at the pervert I moved across to the right hand side of the auditorium.

The weirdo had spoiled the fun for I could no longer immerse myself in the film.

 At the interval I got in line to buy an ice cream from the ice cream lady but guess who was standing behind me . . . See Ya . . . I ran down the aisle across to the exit out through a fire door and sprinted back to our little terraced house.

*   *   *

1978

We were short staffed at the ice rink and my duty on that Tuesday morning was to carry out door duties.

Basically I made sure that everyone entering the Ice Rink had a ticket or a pass.

Tuesdays and Thursdays were reserved for the figure skaters that meant; serious minded skaters who were practising their ice skating skills as seen on TV programmes like *Dancing On Ice.*

No Ice hockey skates - which meant no tearaways on the ice . . . **decorum** was the word.

During my time at Streatham Ice Rink I was fortunate enough to have been introduced to the figure skating greats such as *Torvill & Dean*, *John Currie* and *Robin Cousins*. Skaters who had done so much to promote Ice skating in Britain and the main reason why Ice Rinks like Streatham had boomed during the seventies and eighties.

My greatest achievement at Streatham Ice Rink took place in 1986 when I organised and put on a special 50th anniversary Gala that I named '50 Golden Years of Streatham Ice Rink'

The Ice Rink's famous Organist David Lowe had been contacted by a friend at the BBC and he suggested that we should do something to celebrate the land mark birthday.

 Fans of the ice rink from all over the world managed to watch a special edition of the BBC's *Nationwide* news bulletin at the peak hour of six pm on a Friday evening: it was all about Streatham Ice Rink's fifty years.

 It ensured that ticket sales for the ensuing Gala were high. The event was staged with help and participation from the country's leading skaters and featured exhibition skating from top international skaters.

 A huge success deserved success for Streatham.

Back to 1978 . . . and I was explaining: As I stood by the tall glass door, feeling a bit tired and uninterested in the mundane manner of the day but my outlook on Tuesdays suddenly changed as I watched a lady walk into the foyer with her son (or perhaps her grandson)

It was Susannah York.

She had her own white figure skates slung over her shoulder as she held the hand of the nine year old boy and approached the ticket kiosk, she looked as great in real life as she did on the big silver screen.

"Stop" I shouted.

Ms York stopped in her tracks and stared at me.

Alarmed I am sure at my warning.

She must have thought I was mad,

"Miss York . . ." I yelled and rushed towards her,

She took a step back and pulled the young boy behind her,

"No please . ." I said,

" . . . I didn't mean to alarm you sorry . . . but you must not buy a ticket, it's so good to see you. I mean I am so pleased to see you . . . no I didn't mean that . . . Please . . . be my guest."

Guess what?

Susannah York smiled and chuckled . . . at me!

She thanked me and I escorted her into Streatham Ice Rink. I made sure the young boy got a pair of rental skates and . . . Susannah York and the young lad were regular visitors to Tuesday mornings and . . . she would always greet me by my first name.

Bliss

That really put the memories of the cinema pervert in their righteous place.

*   *   *

Thanks to my great friends on Social Media; Danai and Les and hundreds of others, we have discussed the Ice Rink days on many levels and tried to understand how those magical ingredients created so much happiness and I think it probably goes something like this.

Learning to Ice skate is just as difficult as learning to walk as a toddler and when you finally master it you are in total control of that most wonderful gliding movement that continues for as long as you want it to; no batteries required.

When you add the positives of new friendships and goals that are all brought together under one roof you do actually – without realising – have a brand new family and it never got tiresome.

You get a vibrant sound system and amazing lighting and whether you are on your own or with friends, you feel like you belong there; on that ice pad moving under your own speed and engaging with everyone else that is also happy to be there.

Walking home with soaking wet clothes after being 'sprayed' by another skater was part and parcel of those disco days and watching the speed skaters and the hockey matches felt more normal than watching any other popular sport and guess what? . . . if you felt like joining in there was instant acceptance from the coaching staff to help you participate . . . all that under one roof and so much more . . .

So that is how life was at Streatham Ice Rink, for me and all my friends and all the people who frequented that multi - purpose arena.

Every recreation centre in the world is truly amazing because of the people of all ages who decide for whatever their reason to come together and attend such great social hubs.

I hope that the future Streatham Ice Rinks of this world are fortunate enough to be frequented by such wonderful characters like the ones I knew and … thanks to social media; still keep in contact with.

 Many of us still live in or pass through Streatham and its old sights and venues.

I don't know about you . . . but I still shed a fond tear or two.

Thanks for the friendship.

Thanks for the memories, with very special thanks to Jack and Peter Iandoli to Alec and Kathy Goldstone and all our friends past and present.

The End (for now)

30229624R00092

Printed in Great
Britain
by Amazon